John Buchan was born in 1875 in P(
Childhood holidays were spent in the I
great love. His passion for the Scottish _____ ,
his writing. He was educated at Glasgow University and Brasenose
College, Oxford, where he was President of the Union.

Called to the Bar in 1901, he became Lord Milner's assistant
private secretary in South Africa. In 1907 he was a publisher with
Nelson's. In World War I he was a *Times* correspondent at the
Front, an officer in the Intelligence Corps and adviser to the War
Cabinet. He was elected Conservative MP in one of the Scottish
Universities' seats in 1927 and was created Baron Tweedsmuir in
1935. From 1935 until his death in 1940 he was Governor
General of Canada.

Buchan is most famous for his adventure stories. High in
romance, these are peopled by a large cast of characters, of which
Richard Hannay is his best known. Hannay appears in *The Thirty-
nine Steps*. Alfred Hitchcock adapted it for the screen. A TV series
featured actor Robert Powell as Richard Hannay.

FICTION	NON-FICTION
THE BLANKET OF THE DARK	AUGUSTUS
CASTLE GAY	THE CLEARING HOUSE
THE COURTS OF THE MORNING	GORDON AT KHARTOUM
THE DANCING FLOOR	THE KING'S GRACE
THE FREE FISHERS	THE MASSACRE OF GLENCOE
THE GAP IN THE CURTAIN	MONTROSE
GREENMANTLE	OLIVER CROMWELL
GREY WEATHER	SIR WALTER RALEIGH
THE HALF-HEARTED	SIR WALTER SCOTT
THE HOUSE OF THE FOUR WINDS	
HUNTINGTOWER	
THE ISLAND OF SHEEP	
JOHN BURNET OF BARNS	
THE LONG TRAVERSE	
A LOST LADY OF OLD YEARS	
MIDWINTER	
THE PATH OF THE KING	
THE POWER-HOUSE	
PRESTER JOHN	
A PRINCE OF THE CAPTIVITY	
THE RUNAGATES CLUB	
SALUTE TO ADVENTURERS	
THE SCHOLAR GIPSIES	
SICK HEART RIVER	
THE THIRTY-NINE STEPS	
THE THREE HOSTAGES	
THE WATCHER BY THE THRESHOLD	
WITCH WOOD	

JOHN BUCHAN
Julius Caesar

HOUSE OF
STRATUS

This edition published in 2008 by House of Stratus, an imprint of Stratus Books Ltd., 21 Beeching Park, Kelly Bray, Cornwall, PL17 8QS, UK.

www.houseofstratus.com

Typeset, printed and bound by House of Stratus.

A catalogue record for this book is available from the British Library.

ISBN 07551-170-4-2

TO
MY FRIEND
AIRCRAFTSMAN T E SHAW

CONTENTS

INTRODUCTION

Two main types may be discerned in the inner circle of human greatness. One is the cyclopean architect, the daimonic force who swings the world into a new orbit, whose work is as plain as the result of some convulsion of nature, but whose personality is hard to discover behind the colossal facade of his achievements, and at whose mental processes we can only guess. Such are the conquerors, the men of the sword, the Alexanders and Charlemagnes. The second is the man whose business is directly with souls, the thinker, the priest, and the prophet. His influence is to be looked for in no solid concrete creation, but must be traced through a thousand intricate channels, like the advent of spring. The minds of such we know fully, for the mind was their tool, and the mind of man was the object on which they wrought.

Caesar belongs to neither type. He performed the greatest constructive task ever achieved by human hands. He drew the habitable earth into an empire which lasted for five centuries, and he laid the foundations of a fabric of law and government which is still standing after two thousand years. He made the world possible for the Christian faith, so that there was reason in the mediaeval belief which saw in him a Bishop and a Father of the Church. He gave humanity order and peace, and thereby prepared the ground for many precious seeds. His genius as soldier and law-maker is amply proven. The greatest of poets believed him to have been 'the noblest man that ever lived in the tide of times.' But although we can come under the spell of his magnificence and appraise his character, we cannot probe to its inner springs. About the mind of this man, his inmost thoughts and dreams, there is still a mystery. We know the things that he did, but not why he did them.

He emerges from the clouds of mythology, lives his life in clear air, and then disappears in a divine mist. He was sprung from the ancient kings of Rome, and had the Goddess of Love herself as an ancestress. Before his death he was regarded by the Roman populace as a god, and later he was believed to have literally ascended into Heaven. To the Middle Ages he was a vast cosmic portent out of which men devised miracle plays; fairy legend laid hold of him and made him, by Morgan la Fay, the father of Oberon the fairy king. But between these banks of vapour his life is as clear as a bright autumn day. The exact nature of his civil and military exploits is rarely in doubt. We have his own writings to guide us, and those of his marshals, and Cicero's many letters and speeches. We know much about his manners and tastes, and we have authentic busts. He is easier to picture than any other figure of classical antiquity.

Yet mystery remains. We have no contemporary who read his thoughts, for the book of Asinius Pollio is lost to us, and Cicero is too deeply concerned with himself to have space for the psychology of others. The biographies which we possess, like those of Plutarch and Suetonius, came a century or two later, and they were the work of writers with a bias, as if the life of Cromwell had been written by Izaak Walton and Dr Johnson. Moreover, Caesar was one who did not trouble to reveal himself to the world except by deeds. He went his smiling way among men, hiding his thoughts behind a gentle and impenetrable courtesy. The bust in the British Museum, the noblest presentment of the human countenance known to me, tells us much, but not all. The broad, full brow and the sinewy neck we take for granted, but what of the strange contraction of the jaws, and the fine, almost feminine, moulding of the lips and chin? Caesar is the only great man of action, save Nelson, who has in his face something of a woman's delicacy. The features conceal more than they reveal. As in the hour of death at the base of Pompey's statue, he has muffled his face. It may be permitted to attempt once again to draw aside the folds of the cloak.

CHAPTER 1

The Republic in Decay

The Roman republic at the start was a community of yeomen dwelling in and around a fortified town. Sovereignty lay with the whole body of citizens, from whom came the laws and the selection of magistrates, and no burgess, save during his tenure of office, had privilege or authority beyond the others. Based upon a disciplined family life, the early commonwealth had the integrity of a household, every member was soldier and law-giver, and every member was a potential commander in the field and civilian chief. But as the state from its military prowess advanced in wealth and added to its domains, this simplicity disappeared, and a privileged class arose, greater in riches and in inherited prestige than the rest. These were the Patricians, the descendants of the first founders, and the early history of the republic is the history of the strife between them and the unprivileged Plebeians. The quarrel was settled by the creation within the whole body of the Populus of a separate corporation, the Plebs, with its own officers and a concurrent right of law-making. The constitution was meticulously balanced, not only as between the Populus and the Plebs, but as between the Populus and the leaders whom it elected. All offices were unpaid and temporary, and each officer was given a colleague whose veto could paralyse his activities, while above them was the Senate, the permanent council of the state. Hence, except for certain legal purposes, the distinction between Patrician and Plebeian lost its importance. A new mixed nobility governed the republic, an aristocracy based on wealth, efficiency, and the inclusion of great officers of state in its ancestry.

Slowly this compact and resolute community enlarged its bounds. It conquered its Latin neighbours and made the other Italian states its docile allies. Before the lapse of six centuries from its foundation it had been forced to carry its arms far beyond the bounds of Italy, and to bring many foreign peoples, as the legal phrase went, 'in arbitratu, dicione, potestate, amicitiave populi Romani.' By the beginning of the third century before Christ, Rome had become mistress of the Italian peninsula. In the second century the Macedonian and Punic wars had given her Greece and part of North Africa, and by its close she controlled the whole Mediterranean basin and had fallen heir to the greater part of the empire of Alexander. It was an uneasy suzerainty; her new empire was not integrated under any plan, but presented a baffling collection of diverse polities, and even in Italy itself there was no complete acceptance of her rule. The frontiers, too, were still fluid; in the east, Anatolia was a muttering volcano; beyond it, stretching into the dim spaces of Asia, the Parthian power hung like a thunder cloud; while to the north and west lay the unconquered Celtic and Germanic peoples, whose strange tumultuous mass movements had already threatened her very citadel.

This miraculous expansion was achieved rather by accident than by design. A bold and adventurous spirit like the elder Scipio accepted it with open eyes; but the majority of Romans drifted into it by the sheer compulsion of facts, and there were not wanting men like the elder Cato, who would have confined the Roman rule to Italy. But the pressure of circumstance was too strong; conquests brought wealth, and money is a potent argument; the governing aristocracy became rapidly a plutocracy, its appetite growing with each success. In spite of itself the City-state had become the Great-state.

Yet it retained its antique urban constitution, and the forms which had sufficed for a simple community of farmers were strained so as to embrace the inhabited globe. A city with less than half a million free denizens, a city-state with less than a million voters, attempted to control a greater domain than Alexander's. This paradox was matched by the paradox of the constitution itself. The Roman people reigned but did not govern. The permanent governing power was the Senate, which had steered the republic through the great wars of defence and conquest. It prepared the laws for the people to ratify, and received into its body the magistrates whom the people elected. By the end of the second century it had become virtually an oligarchy of office-holding families. The Assembly, the legal sovereign, had less actual power than a king in the most limited of monarchies. The senatorial oligarchy, who gave themselves the name of Optimates as embodying all the traditional wisdom of the state, were resolute to retain their privileges, and exclude from their ranks all 'new men' who did not come within that sacred circle which could count curule magistrates in its ancestry. As against it there grew up the party of the Populares, who laid the emphasis on the rule of the whole community; but the opposition was illusory, since they too accepted the machine of the old city-state, which made impossible any serious popular government. How could the whole nation assemble in the narrow limits of the Field of Mars, and vote intelligently on a question obscurely propounded by a magistrate? The power of the people lay only in the election of officials, and not in decisions on policy, and elections tended consequently to be a sordid business of personal influence and lavish bribes. A superior magistracy carried with it the government of one of the overseas provinces, and therefore ample opportunities for enrichment; so the functions of the sovereign people were limited to deciding which members of the oligarchy should be given the privilege and in return for what largesse.

Such a constitution would have worked badly in a small self-contained state. There was no easy mechanism of change, and emergencies had to be met by special appointments and by the suspension of laws – expedients which brought the normal law into contempt. The Senate was perpetually, as Tacitus said of Pompey, 'suarum legum auctor ac subversor.' The administration of the foreign domains was little better than a farce. There was no principle of provincial government, and therefore no continuity; everything depended upon the character of the proconsul. There was no permanent civil service at home or abroad, and the ordering of the city itself was as casual as the administration of Greece and Macedonia. As for public finance it was naked chaos. The state domains and the tribute due from foreign possessions were farmed out to joint-stock companies of Roman capitalists. The Roman polity at the close of the second century before Christ has been described not unfairly as 'government by the unpaid aristocrat and exploitation by the irresponsible profiteer.'

In such a commonwealth much will depend upon the armed forces. Rome had travelled far from the citizen militia which had built up her greatness. There is no such guarantee for sobriety in public affairs as the fact that any citizen may have to risk his life for the policy which he approves. Armies were now no longer conscript but volunteer, and the soldier was a professional, enlisted under a particular general for a particular campaign, and looking to that general for his reward. His loyalty was owed to him and not to the state, and the *sacramentum*, or military oath, was his charter. Such an army of mercenaries put into the hand of a great commander a most potent weapon, for it was his personal following and could be readily used to cut the knots in political dispute.

If the ancient polity of Rome was proving inadequate to the new duties laid upon it, the spirit which had created that polity and had given it value was rapidly disappearing. The strength of the antique Roman character lay in its narrowness, its Calvinistic sense of sin, its austere conception of civic and personal duty, its

4

hardy asceticism, its rigid family ties. Such a type could not adjust itself to novel conditions; if the traditional sanctions were once weakened the whole fabric must crumble. The new Roman had not the *gravitas* of his ancestors. The opening up to him of Greece and the East had induced new tastes and appetites, and he had fallen under the spell of both the refinements and the luxuries of the Hellenic world. His strict domestic discipline had broken down, and popular opinion admitted extravagances and vices which would have been unthinkable in the old republic. The traditional *pietas* had largely gone, for Greek philosophy was a sceptical dissolvent of the antique religion. What had once been a faith which governed the homeliest incidents of daily life was now only an antiquarian tradition retained for political purposes. The masses fell back upon blind superstition and exotic cults, and the finer minds sought a refuge in the cosmic speculations of the Greek thinkers, or, like Lucretius, in an austere intellectualism which was a near neighbour to despair. A vague belief in the *anima mundi* had not the same influence on conduct as the concrete faith which was intertwined with household laws. Doubtless there were many both among the patricians and the new middle class who still stood in the old ways, for it is easy to paint too dark a picture of Roman decadence. There were still those to whom the home was a dominant loyalty, and who could say with Cicero – 'Hic arae sunt, hic foci, hic di penates; hic sacra, religiones, caerimoniae continentur.' But for the bulk of the people the past was dead, and they had to face new seas and tides without chart or compass.

The older aristocracy, at the close of the second century, had either relapsed upon a barren pride of birth, drawing in their skirts from an unfamiliar world, or had joined with the 'new men' in the frantic race for wealth. It was the rise of these new men that made the chief feature of the epoch. The Equites, the upper middle class, were the great capitalists of the day. They farmed the state rents and taxes, contracted for the armies, made fortunes in the slave trade, and controlled the banks. Usury was one of the main industries of the Roman world, which speculated on a gigantic scale and was perpetually in debt. To be a banker was the readiest way to fortune. The big joint-stock companies made advances to rich and poor, accepted deposits, and by means of a cheque system transferred cash throughout the empire. They played a useful, indeed an indispensable, part, but they were the main agents in furthering the systematic plunder of the provinces by Roman officials, and in encouraging the insensate speculative mania in Rome herself. They were responsible for the fact that half the people were always in debt, and that the cry of debt-repudiation was the stock-in-trade of every demagogue.

Below the business class came the Roman populace, now very mixed in blood. Paying no taxes and bearing no civic burdens, they had nevertheless their votes in the Assembly and were a dangerous powder-magazine for sparks. A city like Rome had no corn lands within easy reach, transport was difficult and slow, so it became necessary to organise the food supply. The import and supply of cheap food was a necessity if the people were not to starve, and it was only a step from selling corn below the market-price to distributing it free. The masses lived in huge warrens of slum-tenements (a favourite investment of the new capitalists), and spent most of their time in the Forum and in the streets. The old free artificers and tradesmen were fewer in number, since the great houses with their slaves and freedmen were self-contained economic units, and most of the workers were unskilled labourers. The police system was rudimentary, and both life and property were insecure. The poorer freemen of Rome had become little better than parasites, living largely on doles, kept amused by free shows, accustomed to rioting with little police interference. No demagogue had ever better material for his purpose, so small wonder that demagogy became a recognised profession. The masses were told that they were the real rulers of the world, and, since their life was brutish and uncertain, they would readily welcome any revolution which might give them the fruits of that rule. They had nothing to lose by disorder and much to gain.

At the bottom of the social pyramid were the hordes of slaves, that canker of the ancient world. Slavery under the old rural regime had been often a tolerable rule of life with its own dignity; but in the welter of the new capitalist society it was an unmitigated evil. The slaves crowded the freemen out of the arts and crafts, and many of them acquired a potent secret influence over their masters and the conduct of private and public business. In town and country alike they did all the menial work and most of the superior management. In Rome itself they numbered over a quarter of a million. They were of every type from the artistic and scholarly Greeks to the roughs of the cattle ranches. Here was a vast population of which the state had no control, a private army over which the masters had powers of life and death, a race who owed no loyalty to the commonwealth. Such an element was not only a perpetual danger to the state, but it perverted the moral sense of the best citizens. In it we may find the chief source of the instability of ancient societies, and of that coarseness of fibre which offends us even in what we most deeply admire. With slavery as a sinister background there could be no true *humanitas*.

The close of the second century was, therefore, for Rome a time of unsettlement and doubt, when to the wisest minds it seemed that the commonwealth had entered upon a decline. It was a period of immense material progress. Rome had most of the world at her feet, and her citizens were growing rich with the accumulated wealth of eastern despotisms. The little town of tufa and stucco, sprawled over its many hills, was rapidly becoming a city of marble. But behind this splendid facade there were signs of decay. The great patrician houses produced either haughty and half-witted reactionaries – 'homines praeposteri' or degenerates who joined in the scramble for wealth. The middle classes had built up a capitalistic system which was oppressing the overseas provinces, ruining the free agriculture of Italy, and winding the whole people in coils of debt. A false imperialism, based on the interests of the capitalists, regarded the provinces as mere milch-cows from which tribute could be drawn. In Rome herself, a mongrel population, petted and pampered and yet eternally on the verge of famine, had taken the place of the old stalwart freemen, while the slave masses were a perilous undigested element in the body politic. Worse still, the ancient moral standards of personal continence and discipline and of public loyalty were gravely weakened. The aristocracy had become an oligarchy and largely a plutocracy; the Senate was losing the power to govern; and the whole machinery of the state was cracking under burdens for which it had not been designed.

To wise men it was becoming clear that three reforms were overdue. The central government must be put into stronger and cleaner hands; the power of the capitalists to mismanage the public finances and oppress the masses must be curbed; and some means must be found of organising the new empire not as a bundle of alien tributary states, but as one great organic polity. These ideas had scarcely yet come to birth, but they were in the germ, and they meant the renunciation of the former Roman doctrines of government and the narrow bounds of the city-state. The conquests of Alexander and the lessons taught by the Greek political theorists pointed the same moral, for they involved the conception of the earth as one universal society, in which all free men were equal citizens, and of the state not as a city but as a cosmopolis. They involved something more – some opportunism about the nature of the central power, and the abandonment of the old republican rigidity. It was plain to the wise that the affairs of Rome, for all her apparent splendour, were moving fast to a crisis, and the words spoken by Cicero half a century later were already being whispered in secret: 'No issue can be looked for from discords among the leading men except either universal ruin, or the rule of a conqueror, or a monarchy.'

CHAPTER 2

The Forerunners

In the last century of the republic there was no dearth of would-be reformers. The ills of the state were not hard to diagnose, but there was little agreement about the cure. There were the idolaters of the past, the antiquarians, who tried to achieve the impossible and revive creeds and manners that had gone. There were the enlightened aristocrats who strove to marry what was best in the old and new cultures, and to create a type of Roman in whom a liberal philosophy should not weaken the ancient fibre. Such a one was the younger Scipio, the perfect example of a Roman gentleman, wise, moderate, urbane, clear-sighted; but he was as ineffective to cure the mischief as was Lord Falkland to stem the tide of the English Civil War. The trouble needed more drastic surgery.

The first of the rough surgeons were the two Gracchi, the grandsons of the great Scipio Africanus. The elder, Tiberius, who was born in 163, grappled with the eternal land question, and as tribune carried an agrarian law to make state lands, illegally held by the big landowners, available for settlement by landless citizens. When the opposition to his policy proved too strong to be met by constitutional methods, he summoned a bodyguard from the pavement, and at the age of thirty was crushed in that arbitrament of force to which he had appealed. He tried to build his authority on the popular Assembly, but no serious democracy could be based on what had become a farcical piece of mechanism. Gaius, the younger brother, carried on the work of the dead Tiberius, but with a bolder hand and a wider vision. As tribune he stretched the tribunician power to its extreme limits, and presently passed beyond them into what was constitutionally rebellion. There is scarcely a conception of the later reformers which is not to be found in the policy of Gaius Gracchus. His aim seems to have been to create a perpetual magistracy based on the tribunician power, to transfer the practical sovereignty from the Senate to the popular Assembly and the middle classes, and to replace the city-state by an Italian nation. But such a course meant a defiance of the existing law, and he had not the force behind him for successful revolution. The varied antagonisms which he had roused coalesced against him, and his end was a violent death. One lesson stood out from the failure of the brothers for all to read. For a reformer a bodyguard from the pavement was not enough; he must have behind him a great army.

Presently appeared the popular leader with the army, but he was not the stuff of which revolutionary statesmen are made. Gaius Marius, the son of a Latin farmer, rose from the ranks to be commander-in-chief against Jugurtha, and became consul fourteen years after the death of the younger Gracchus. He recast the army on a democratic basis, rolled back the invasion of the Cimbri and the Teutons, and became the virtual dictator of Rome. But Marius was only a peasant of genius, slow-witted, inelastic, a good soldier but a blundering politician. Seven times he was consul, and when he returned to Rome as conqueror he was naturally called to the leadership of the Populares. But he was in the hands of demagogues, who professed to carry out the dream of Gaius Gracchus without comprehending their true purpose. The uneasy alliance dissolved, Marius dropped out of public life, and the senatorial party won the triumph which falls to those who know their own minds. An attempt at reform from the side of the moderate aristocrats succeeded no better, and its leader, Livius

Drusus, went the way of the Gracchi. But the silencing of protesting voices could not bring peace; the incompetence of the Senate, the greed of the capitalists, the unrest of the Roman mob, and the discontent of the disenfranchised Italians remained; and at the close of the first decade of the last century before Christ all Italy was in the throes of insurrection.

Some reconstruction was inevitable, even if it were only temporary and partial, and to this task a remarkable man set his hand. Lucius Cornelius Sulla was sprung from one of the oldest of the patrician houses, and had spent his youth as a dissolute man of fashion and an amateur of art and letters. But the war with Jugurtha revealed to him his exceptional military talent, and thenceforth he was above all things a soldier, with a soldier's contempt for political squabbles. The honours of the last phase of the North African campaign fell to him, he played a leading part in the defeat of the Cimbri and the Teutons and in quelling the Italian revolt, and earlier he had, as propraetor in Asia, patched up a truce with Mithridates of Pontus. He was consul when Mithridates took the field again and crossed the Bosphorus and overran Greece, and he was appointed to command against the most formidable foe that Rome had known since Hannibal. But he was suspected by the popular party, and by a decree of the people the charge of the war against Mithridates was entrusted to Marius.

Sulla did not hesitate. He had little respect for aristocracy, capitalists or rabble, but he was determined to defend his country, and he had no belief in his old leader. He marched his six legions on Rome, took the city, and lit his watch-fires in the marketplace, while Marius fled to the salt marshes of Minturnae. He proceeded to put together an interim constitution, the basis of which was the degradation of the Assembly and the restoration of the right of initiative to the Senate. Otherwise he allowed the Gracchan innovations to stand. Then, leaving as he well knew no secure settlement behind him, he embarked his legions for the East. This contemptuous grandee, with his piercing blue eyes and blotched face 'like a floury mulberry,' was cynical about all things but one; he hated cant and bungling, and was resolute to face realities. The major problem was to crush Mithridates, and he was ready to let politics at Rome drift into chaos so long as this task was accomplished. So with 30,000 men and no fleet he set out against a conqueror who had command of the sea and of armies unnumbered, and already controlled every Roman domain east of the Adriatic except a fragment of Macedonia.

Sulla was absent for four years, and meantime Rome was in anarchy. The popular party, with Cinna at its head, repealed the Sullan acts, old Marius returned from exile, and there followed a great massacre of opponents. Marius, savage, drunken and now half insane, passed in 86 to a dishonoured death, and till 84 Cinna was virtually tyrant of Rome. He had no serious policy, beyond revenge upon his enemies and sops to the mob, but under his rule the rights of citizenship were finally confirmed to all Italy south of the Po. Anxiously he kept his eyes on the East, where month by month Sulla was moving steadily on his career of conquest. Nothing perturbed that extraordinary man. When Rome sent a general to replace him, he won over the general's troops, and he made his own armies his loyal personal following. He finished his immediate task, made terms with Mithridates, and in 83 returned to Italy, with a veteran army and ample treasure. Some of the ablest of the officers who had taken service under Cinna joined him, like the young Pompey and the young Marcus Crassus, the government levies melted before him, and in a battle at the very gates of Rome the last stand of the Populares was broken. Sulla was made dictator for such time as he pleased to hold office, with absolute power over the lives of Romans and the laws of Rome.

He was too humorous and too cynical to be cruel for cruelty's sake, and the terrible proscription which followed had a reasoned purpose – to get rid for good of troublesome opponents, and to discourage for the future performances like those of Marius and Cinna. Then, before retiring to the leisure which he had amply earned and the pleasures which were his main interest in life, he set to work to remake the constitution. He despised alike the mob and the aristocracy, but concluded that the latter was 'the more natural beast of the twain,' so the object of his changes was to aggrandise the Senate, teach the middle class their place, and put the rabble in bonds. One thing he did not touch; he left the Roman citizenship to the Italians, for he saw the folly of again stirring up that secular strife. Also, like the Gracchi, he established many new colonies, chiefly of his former soldiers, who, he believed, would act as a guard for his new regime. He increased the numbers of the Senate, made it an oligarchy of officials by confining its membership to those who had held the higher magistracies, and secured to it the legislative initiative. He established a strict *cursus honorum,* and weakened the tribunate by imposing a heavy fine for the improper use of the veto, and laying it down, that a tribune was disqualified from standing for a higher office. He abolished the corn doles. He took the jury-courts away from the Equites and restored them to the Senate, and he dealt a heavy and just blow at the capitalists by putting an end to the farming of the revenues of Asia and making each province levy its own tribute.

There was much that was good in his reconstruction. If Sulla is to be credited with any principle, it was a belief in the republic, and he sincerely thought that he was restoring republican institutions. He had given the Roman oligarchy a last chance. It was not an aristocratic restoration, for there was no real aristocracy left, but it was an attempt to create an efficient bureaucracy backed by an efficient police. It solved no one of Rome's greater problems, such as the relation of the new mercenary armies to the civil power, or the absorption of the provinces into the Roman polity. But Sulla was not concerned with the dim future; it was enough for him to set the old machine going again, so that he could withdraw to the life of ease which he loved. A cynic to the core, he feared danger no more than he feared the mouthings of the demagogues. Though many thousands desired his death, he laid down his dictator's power and retired calmly to the life of the sportsman, the epicure, and the literary dilettante. A year later, fortunate to the last, he died peacefully in his bed. All Italy stood around his pyre, and the women of Rome mourned him for a year.

The Sullan reconstruction left, as I have said, the main blemishes in the state untouched. It put the government into the hands of an official oligarchy who had lost the talent for government, and had in any case at their disposal a most unworkable machine. The narrow city-state had gone, but a body of citizens scattered throughout the Italian peninsula were no better fitted to administer an empire. Moreover, the credulous and undisciplined urban mob had still ample power to make mischief. It did not take from the capitalists the opportunities of public plunder. It did not diminish the opposition between Optimates and Populares, between those who had and those who had not, but the opposition had become merely opportunist and had no serious basis of principle. Cicero defined the Optimates as those who said and did what pleased the best men, but the word 'best' was equivocal. There were among the Optimates stiff relic-worshippers, republicans of the old rock, who had forgotten nothing and learned nothing; but there were also moderate men, especially among the jurists, who saw the necessity of reform. In the ranks of the Populares were shallow radicals who worshipped phrases and bankrupts who hungered for revolution, but there were also many solid citizens who resented the contempt of the aristocrats, and all the classes proscribed by Sulla, and the aspiring young men who always draw to an opposition. One thing was clear. Politics had become the profession of every ambitious Roman, and everywhere political clubs and coteries were springing up like weeds. Through politics alone a man could win to wealth and high civil and military command.

Such was the view of a young cadet of the great Julian house just back from the East, whose candid eyes were now surveying the Roman scene.

CHAPTER 3

The Youth of Caesar

This young man, Gaius Julius Caesar, was born on the 12th of July 102, the year when at Aquae Sextiae Marius checked the advance of the Teutons in Gaul. He belonged to a branch of the patrician Julian family, which traced descent from Aeneas and so from the gods, and his grandmother Marcia claimed the blood of Ancus Marcius, the fourth of the early Roman kings. His mother, Aurelia, was also of the inner circle of the aristocracy. His branch of the Julii had held in recent generations many high public offices, but had produced no figure of the first importance. They were patricians of the moderate school, and his aunt Julia had broken with the traditions of her caste and married the plebeian Marius.

When he was not yet eighteen his father died, for the Caesars were a short-lived race. His mother lived for thirty years more, long enough to see her son the conqueror of Gaul, and it would appear that Aurelia was the chief formative influence of his youth. To the end of her life she was his friend and counsellor, a gentler figure than the mother of the Gracchi, but with much of the antique Roman discipline. Of his education we know little. He had as tutor not a Greek but a Cisalpine Gaul, but, according to the fashion, most of his training must have been on Greek lines, since the Latin schools of rhetoric were closed when he was ten years old. For Hellenic culture he cherished an abiding love; when in 48 Athens surrendered to him after Pharsalus, he spared the people 'because of their dead'; nevertheless he was always more Roman than Greek in his habits of thought. He dabbled in literature, and wrote a tragedy and some boyish love-songs, which long afterwards Augustus took pains to suppress, believing that they would not add to his fame; he also acquired two hobbies which never left him, astronomy and an eager curiosity about the undiscovered regions of the globe, and he pored over the Alexandrian geographers.

Quite early he seems to have developed an interest in politics, and to have leaned, through the influence of his mother, and of the Marian circle to which his aunt's marriage introduced him, to the side of the Populares. When he was sixteen Marius and Cinna nominated him as *flamen dialis,* or priest of Jupiter, and his father, who was then living, did not object. When he was nineteen he married Cornelia, Cinna's daughter, a bold step, for Cinna's power was crumbling and the avenging Sulla was on the seas. A year later his cousin, the younger Marius, died at Praeneste, and had his head spiked in the marketplace to the accompaniment of Sulla's caustic epigram, 'One must first become an oarsman before handling the rudder.' Presently the conqueror set about rearranging Roman society. Pompey obediently divorced his wife at Sulla's command and accepted the hand of his stepdaughter. But the young Caesar defied him. He refused to divorce Cinna's daughter, with the consequence that he lost his priesthood and his wife's dowry, and was compelled to hide in fever-stricken nooks of the Apennines, being saved only by the influence of his mother's house and the intercession of the college of the Vestal Virgins. It was a bold act for a young man of twenty, but Caesar never throughout his life knew the meaning of fear.

His politics were still a boy's politics, based on personalities and romance. Old Marius his kinsman, of whose ugly side he knew little, had been the hero of his youth, and his cousin, the younger

Marius, was a picturesque adventurer. A boy takes sides in any quarrel, and Caesar's side was predestined. He was brought daily into contact with the leaders of the Populares, and also with the rising capitalist classes. His father had tried to marry him to a financier's daughter, and his niece had espoused one Gaius Octavius, the son of a rich country banker. He heard the talk of these people, their complaints of the inefficiency of the Senate and the blundering arrogance of the oligarchy, and it sank deep into his mind. He may also have suffered personally from the boorishness of the elder senatorians and the raffish insolence of the younger. But he was a young man with whom no one took liberties, very courteous and with a pleasant wit of his own, but not inclined to air his opinions or reveal his heart. Cicero, who knew him as a boy, makes fun in his letters of every other contemporary, but he never trifles with Caesar.

From earliest youth he cast a curious spell over all who met him. He had a genius for attracting people to him, and doing kindnesses with a graciousness which left no sting. Already he was schooling himself to discover men's souls and play on them as on an instrument of music. He ranked as tall among the small-boned Romans – perhaps five foot eight; he was very slim, but his figure was wiry and athletic, and he excelled in swimming, riding, and swordsmanship. In a gluttonous age he was noted for his moderation in both food and wine. He dressed carefully and always kept his body in hard condition. His head was large, beautifully shaped, and set on a sinewy neck; his forehead was broad, his nose strong and aquiline, his complexion a healthy pallor, and his eye dark and piercing like an eagle's. He was capable of feats of great endurance, but constitutionally he was always a little delicate, suffering from recurring bouts of fever. Altogether a formidable young man, whose eyes revealed nothing and missed nothing, a puzzle alike to strenuous *arrivistes* like Cicero and to the apolaustic youth of his own class. He was biding his time and forming himself, for he remembered Sulla's gibe about his cousin Marius.

When he escaped the Sullan proscription he went to the East for his term of military service. He served under one of Sulla's lieutenants at the siege of Mytilene, and won the 'civic crown' for saving a soldier's life. He was despatched on duty to Bithynia, whose king, Nicomedes, had been restored to the throne. A quarter of a century later Roman gossip credited him with indulging at Nicomedes' court in orgies of oriental vice. There is no reason to believe the slander, for it was one regularly spread in the Roman world about every great figure in public life, just as charges of incontinence were automatically levied by the Puritans against every Cavalier. Exotic debaucheries had no attraction for Caesar, and it is to be noted that in a plea for certain Bithynians, made when he was Pontifex Maximus, he spoke most frankly and naturally of his dealings with Nicomedes, which scarcely suggests a guilty conscience. After Mytilene he joined the fleet of Servilius Isauricus in its campaign against the Cilician pirates. While there he heard of Sulla's death, and returned to Rome to see if the political world was now ripe for his entrance.

He arrived in time for the abortive rebellion of Lepidus, a light-headed enterprise with which, though solicited by young Cinna his brother-in-law, he would have nothing to do. Instead he turned to the law-courts. He was not rich, but Aurelia had carefully conserved his inheritance, and he had enough to launch him in public life. He prosecuted the ex-proconsul of Macedonia on a charge of extortion, and, though he failed to secure a conviction, he won a certain amount of repute. Next year he attacked another malefactor of the same type and failed again. Clearly he required more training, so, characteristically, he went to seek it where it could best be got. At the age of twenty-eight he sailed for Rhodes to study under Apollonius Molo, who had been Cicero's master. He had no cause to lose heart because of his comparative failure in the law-courts. Cicero, who had a complete professional training, undertook no political case till he was thirty-six.

But the next year was not to be one of academic study, but an interlude of wild adventure. On the way to Rhodes he was captured by pirates. While his friends were sent off to raise the necessary ransom, Caesar remained as a hostage, and for twenty-eight days was the life and soul of the company. He promised cheerfully to hang them all, a promise which he faithfully kept, when the ransom arrived and he could hire ships at Miletus. Apollonius must have had an unsatisfactory pupil, for the next we hear is of Caesar raising troops to repel the new invasion of Mithridates. Meantime, in his absence he had been elected through the influence of his mother's family to a place in the college of *pontifices,* and he felt that, in Napoleon's phrase, he had done enough 'pour chauffer la gloire' and should return home. He knew that he would get short shrift if pirates captured him a second time, so he hired a vessel which could outsail any pirate craft, and reached Rome at the end of 74. There he won his first elective office, that of military tribune, and as such he may have served against Spartacus in the Slave insurrection which presently broke out. He was living in a modest establishment with his mother and his wife, improving daily in his oratory in spite of his high-pitched voice, and circumspectly surveying the political field. He was now entering his thirtieth year.

CHAPTER 4

The Party Game

The first two years of Caesar's life in Rome as an aspirant to a political career gave him ample material for thought. The Sullan regime had produced the inevitable reaction, for it contented nobody except the inner circle of the Senate; the more enlightened of the aristocracy, the lawyers, the middle class and the mob were alike dissatisfied. The opposition of the Populares became suddenly respectable. The supple mind of the young Caesar, which may once have dreamed of a Periclean democracy in Rome, a government of the Many who should be also the Best, was now engaged not with visions of a Platonic republic but with the dingy realities of the 'cesspool of Romulus.' He was clear about two things – that the aristocracy was no longer fit to govern, and that the traditional constitution of Rome was inadequate to its new duties. But it seems to me idle to hold, with some of his hero-worshippers, that he had already conceived a plan of reconstruction, and that he worked throughout his life on the dream 'that pleased his boyish thought.' That is not how a realistic intelligence behaves, and Caesar was the supreme realist of history. He was ambitious to succeed in the fashionable game of politics, and he cast about him for the best methods.

These were years of war. The Slave revolt under Spartacus was brought to an end by Marcus Crassus. The ex-Marian Sertorius, one of the most enlightened and attractive figures in Roman records, was at long last crushed in Spain by Pompey. Mithridates was checked in his conquering progress by Lucius Lucullus, who was making war with a free hand and performing miracles of which political hatred was to deprive him of the credit. Caesar saw that in the chaos of the Roman state the decisive word would lie with the man who had an army at his back. Especially was he interested in the commander in Spain, who was only four years his senior. Pompey was the luckiest of mortals. Sulla had saluted him as Imperator when he was twenty-three, and had called him 'the Great,' and he had been permitted the honour of a triumph at the age of twenty-seven, before he was even a senator. He was a friendly, courteous person, not too puffed up by his successes; handsome in the fleshy Roman way, with melting eyes which women found irresistible. Something might be made of him, for he was not likely to be a docile tool of the Senate. But Caesar had no belief in Pompey's brains. He saw in him talent, but not a trace of genius. If such a man could be a successful soldier, why should not he also win the same laurels and the same power? Moreover, the law and custom of the constitution had been broken by giving Pompey a high command overseas before he had entered on the *cursus honorum*. Marius had been right; the laws were silent when confronted with arms; the only way to get rid of antiquarian lumber was to have an army behind one.

But Caesar realised that he had a long road to travel before he could win Pompey's power, and in the meantime he must use the weapons which lay to his hand. The first of these was the mob – the great mass of the dispossessed and discontented who filled the city kennels. He had no leaning to equalitarian whimsies; the Roman populace was to him a rabble, a squalid thing which had its rights under an antiquated constitution, and might be used to intimidate the oligarchy. Till he could fit himself with a disciplined army he would make shift with a bodyguard from the pavement.

This meant that he must play a large part in the democratic clubs, and make himself a popular favourite. There is no reason to believe that Caesar's debut in the part of a radical leader had any but a tactical motive.

It meant also that he must spend a great deal of money, which his modest patrimony could not provide. Therefore he must cultivate the new monied classes with whom he had already family connections. He must not champion the mob so as to lose the confidence of the capitalists. They were immensely powerful, and it was largely owing to their opposition that Lucullus's brilliant achievements were decried. The most important was Crassus, who had finished the Slave war. Crassus was the eternal type of money-spinner, who in the interests of his business had not attached himself too closely to any party. His fortune ran to several millions sterling, and he had the equivalent of a million and a half invested in land alone. He was a poor speaker, an indifferent soldier, and with little political aptitude, but he was insatiably ambitious. He belonged to an ancient house, and he was also the recognised leader of the rich bourgeoisie, so he naturally believed that he had it in him to head a coalition of what Cicero called 'honest men.' Caesar saw it otherwise. He would make this bustling and not too intelligent plutocrat at once the milch-cow and the stalking-horse of the radicals, and in particular the means of providing his own campaign fund.

The events of the year 70 seemed to favour these views. Pompey and Crassus were consuls, the one in virtue of his military prestige and the other because of his wealth and largesses; each, it was remarked, had legions behind him to enforce his claims, if necessary. Both consuls inclined for the moment against the Optimates. That was the year of the trial of Verres, the restoration of the tribunician power, the recovery by the Equites of a predominant share in the jury-courts and of the farming of the Asian taxes, the revival of the censorship and the consequent striking off of sixty-four members from the roster of the Senate. These changes were brought about by a union of the capitalists and the popular party; Cicero supported them, and Caesar played some part in the restoration of the tribunate, and probably made his first speech in the Forum to a public gathering. The oligarchy was for the moment discredited, and Pompey and Crassus, having undone most of Sulla's work, showed no inclination to go further, but disbanded their forces and retired into private life. The time seemed opportune for the entry into politics of a young man on the popular side.

Two years later Caesar attained his first important office, the quaestorship, in virtue of which he entered the Senate. The post gave him some insight into the details of public business, for it was a kind of secretaryship to the treasury, and involved the management of the municipal supply of corn and water. This year his aunt Julia and his wife Cornelia died, and, in the public eulogies on them which he delivered according to custom, he seized the opportunity of displaying his political colours. He had the bust of Marius carried in Julia's funeral procession, and the people wildly applauded the effigy of the man whose name a decade before they had been forbidden to speak. In his oration Caesar lauded his aunt's divine and royal ancestry, and he proceeded to marry a girl Pompeia, young and well-dowered, who was Sulla's granddaughter. If the role of demagogue was to be his, he was determined that the patrician should not be forgotten.

Presently, according to the Roman ritual of office, he went abroad attached to the propraetor of Farther Spain. This, his first foreign journey on duty, was one of the formative episodes in his life. At Cadiz he is said to have meditated with bitterness that he was now thirty-four and that before that age Alexander had conquered the world. The thought may have quickened his power of reflection and receptivity. He came to understand the meaning of Sertorius' work, for Sertorius was the first Roman to think of provincials as Roman citizens and not as chattels. He fell in love with this land in the West, and saw in its people the stuff of a strong nation. On his way home overland he spent some time in

Cisalpine Gaul, and heard at first hand the grievances of the dwellers north of the Po who were denied the full citizenship. Into his shrewd tactical schemes there came new ideas which stretched far beyond the Roman party game. Rome had a great heritage, human and territorial, outside her city walls, and some day, if the gods were kind, it might fall to his lot to shape it to high purpose.

He returned home early in 67 to find politics at their liveliest. Foreign affairs were in chaos, Mithridates was not conquered, and pirates had so dominated the Mediterranean that the Roman corn supply was imperilled. Pompey, tired of a quiet life, was growing restless, and the people were demanding that some use should be made of the foremost soldier of the day. It was proposed to give him an extraordinary command for three years with an adequate army to suppress piracy, and to recall Lucullus, and when the Senate would have none of it, the tribune Gabinius introduced and carried the measure by a plebiscite. Later, another tribune, Manilius, carried a second plebiscite which entrusted Pompey with the governments of Bithynia, Pontus, and Cilicia, and gave him the sole conduct of the war in the East. These proceedings were a defiance of the custom of the constitution. The burgesses might confirm a special appointment, but hitherto the Senate had made it. But now not only was the Senate roughly set aside, but Pompey was given unlimited financial and military power, which was wholly inconsistent with republican principles. The Senate was furious and impotent, the capitalists were alarmed, and Crassus was sulky; but the need was urgent, for Rome was faced with starvation, and even a moderate like Cicero accepted the Manilian law and spoke in its favour. Caesar and his radicals welcomed it for another reason; they saw that the appointment of Pompey meant the beginning of the end of the old regime.

In 66 Caesar was elected aedile, and took up office on the first day of the following year. Owing to his popular canvassing he had fallen into debt before his quaestorship, and Pompeia's dowry had not cleared his feet. Now with the most expensive of all magistracies on his hands – it meant virtually the administration of the Roman municipality – his borrowings reached a colossal figure. He had to give public games, and in his extravagance he outdid all predecessors, for the very cages of the wild beasts were of silver, and he produced three hundred and twenty pairs of gladiators. He erected costly public buildings, and, greatly daring, he restored and regilded the trophies and statues of Marius on the Capitol. Old Marian veterans wept at the sight, and the young patrician of thirty-seven became as never before the darling of the mob. The result was that he owed some hundreds of thousands of pounds, which he could scarcely have raised if Crassus had not backed his bills.

Caesar had now emerged into the full glare of publicity. To the Senate he was the chief mark for hostility, the real leader of the Populares, vigilant, intrepid, and resourceful. They had feared Pompey, but Pompey was a formal, supine being compared to this audacious meteor. The hope of the old men like Catulus was that he would wear himself out in debaucheries, like other aristocrats who had forsworn their class, and they whispered slanders which have ever since found credence. Most were patently untrue. Caesar was living at the time the life of a man of fashion, but his body was always subject to his mind and his pleasures subordinated to his ambition. He preferred good talk to drunken orgies, and the society of cultivated women to that of the ordinary male glutton. Women indeed had a peculiar fascination for him, and he for them, but he was no casual libertine. Roman morals on this point were of the easiest, for family life was in decay. The elder Cato had the lowest view of the female sex, and the younger Cato was not above divorcing his wife to give her to Hortensius, and remarrying her as Hortensius' well-dowered widow; Cicero plumed himself on flirting with disreputable actresses; Pompey divorced Mucia on account of an intrigue with Caesar, and promptly married the daughter of his wife's seducer. Caesar had a host of women friends, of whom the closest was Servilia, the mother of Marcus Brutus, but there is no evidence that any one of them was his mistress except Pompey's wife. In continence he did not fall below the

25

average standard of his day. As for friends of his own sex, the exigencies of the political game impelled him to have many dealings with blackguards, but he had no taste for raffish company, and even in politics he would have nothing to do with the irredeemable degenerate.

He was tolerant of most men, and able to handle every variety. But there was one exception, Servilia's half-brother, Marcus Porcius Cato, who was seven years his junior, and who followed him steadily at a little distance in the *cursus honorum*. Every type has its anti-type, and to Caesar Cato was eternally antipathetic. He was a man of mediocre intelligence, unshakable self-conceit, and inflexible resolution. New ideas, new facts beat vainly against the shuttered casements of his soul. His moral sense in many ways was no higher than that of others, as he showed in his mission to Cyprus, but to himself he was the one virtuous man in a world of rogues. His strength lay in this sincere conviction, which made him intolerable but also formidable. He was the unyielding reactionary, who may be broken but cannot be bent. His intellect was, as Cicero said of another senator, a mere desert island, 'shore and sky and utter desolation,' but dim as his lights were, he lived stoutly up to them. To Caesar he was the only contemporary whom he genuinely detested; he never forgave him, especially for dying prematurely and so preventing him from punishing his old foe by magnanimity. It was no small achievement to have incurred Caesar's unhesitating dislike.

Meantime in that year of extravagance strange things were going on underground, and Caesar had other relations with Crassus than those of debtor and creditor. The first elected consuls in 66 had been unseated for corrupt practices, and had planned a *coup d'état* to make Crassus dictator and Caesar master of the horse. Crassus was becoming utterly malcontent. He saw his ex-colleague Pompey driving the pirates from the seas, and defeating Mithridates and Tigranes, while he himself languished in wealthy obscurity at home. His irritable ambition revived, and he dreamed of a dictatorship on his own account with Egypt and its treasures as his special province. The conspiracy failed, and the storm blew over, but for Caesar it was a difficult moment. He was very much in Crassus' debt, and dare not quarrel with him, but at the same time he had no wish to break with Pompey, who was still the best card which the radicals held against the Senate. Besides, he was not ready to play a master-stroke, having only reached the aedileship. Nevertheless the abortive conspiracy had brought Crassus nearer to the radicals, and the radicals nearer to what might be called the anarchists, the underground world of bankrupts and libertines who had nothing to lose by violence. Chief of these latter was the late praetor Catiline, who, from the Sullan proscription onwards, had made murder and deeper infamies the daily incidents of his life, and who in 64 was a candidate for the consulship.

In 64, while Pompey was playing the part of conquistador and marching through Syria, the consular elections offered some excitement. Cicero, who had won fame by his prosecution of Verres, the Sullan propraetor of Sicily, and was known as a friend of Pompey, was supported reluctantly by the Optimates, though he had toyed with the Populares and had the confidence of the bourgeoisie of the capital and the country towns. Caesar and Crassus took the side of his rivals Catiline and Antonius, whom they considered with reason to be better tools for their purpose; but the alarm excited by Catiline's appearance was so general that Cicero was elected by a handsome majority, with Antonius as his colleague.

Thus entered into high politics one of the most versatile and gifted of Romans and the supreme master of the Latin tongue. So far Cicero had been only the leader of the bar and a famous man of letters; he had neither wealth nor family behind him, and he was the first to reach the highest office solely by his intellectual attainments. He was honourable, affectionate and loyal, and he had that finest kind of courage which means the habitual suppression of temperamental fears. He saw as clearly as any man the canker in the state, but he could not be its surgeon, for to him the republic was too dear and ancient a thing for a harsh knife. His physical traits, the big head, the thin neck, the mobile mouth, were an index to his character. Sentiment ruled him, the sentiment of a provincial for the old aristocracy, and for the forms which he had been schooled to reverence. He could not take a hand in plucking down a proud class which it had been the dream of his boyhood to enter, for its destruction would take all the pleasure from his laborious career. This innocent snobbishness was joined to an equally innocent vanity, and to a morbid sensitiveness. He was not vain of his true endowments – his oratory, his prose style, his legal and philosophical learning; but the scholar was apt to strut like a peacock after any little success in the alien world of action. He was far more than a mere man of phrases, for in an emergency he could be very bold; but he lacked the two chief qualities of a leader, a knowledge of what he wanted and an eye for things as they were. The first lack made him waver all his life between the upper and the middle classes, between Optimates and Populares, between Caesar and Pompey; the second bound him to a sterile antiquarianism. He wished to restore the rule of all honest men, to link together the Senate and the Equites in a *concordia ordinum*, and to preserve the traditional republican fabric, and he would not admit to himself, except in moments of exasperated candour, that it was a baseless dream. In this he was the exact opposite of Caesar, who was accustomed to look at facts in all their grimness, and who had no sentimental attachment to the aristocracy, since he came from the heart of it and knew its rottenness.

The year 63 was a hard trial for the lawyer-consul. The radicals began briskly with a new agrarian law, promulgated by the tribune Rullus. The measure had no great popular appeal, and Cicero's eloquence easily defeated it. Then they tried another tack. Titus Labienus, one of Caesar's henchmen, indicted for high treason an aged senator, Rabirius, who thirty-seven years before had been concerned in the killing of the tribune Saturninus. This was purely a political demonstration, for the trial was not allowed to come to a verdict, but it was a shrewd assault upon the citadel of the senatorial power; it emphasised for all to mark the tribunes' right of inviolability, and it repudiated the Senate's claim to declare a state of siege, the famous *senatus consultum ultimum*, which put the lives and liberties of the people temporarily in its hands.

There followed a still more notable radical success. The office of Pontifex Maximus fell vacant, an office which carried with it not only high distinction, but considerable revenues, an official residence, and the right of personal immunity, things most valuable to a demagogue who was walking in dangerous ways. Caesar, just over forty, became a candidate against two old and respected senators, Quintus Catulus and Servilius Isauricus. Sulla had placed the election in the hands of the pontifical college itself, but Titus Labienus had it transferred to the Assembly. The contest was an orgy of bribery and added enormously to Caesar's debts, but to the general surprise he was triumphantly elected. He was also chosen as praetor for the coming year.

The law of Rullus, the impeachment of Rabirius, and the candidature for Pontifex Maximus had been open attacks by the radical chiefs upon the senatorial power. But now came an assault on its own account by the extreme left wing, the anarchists from the kennels and the clubs, in which the responsible leaders took no overt part. We may assume that they were aware of the conspiracy, and intended to win repute by checking and disarming it when it had gone a certain length. Catiline was again a candidate for the consulship, but he was now ready to take by violence what he could not get by law. He engineered in Rome and throughout Italy a great plot of the lawless, the disinherited, the bankrupt, and the desperate. At the poll it was proposed to kill Cicero, the presiding consul, and the other candidates, to carry the election of Catiline with the help of armed bands, and thereafter to introduce a millennium of debt-repudiation and public plunder. Cicero got wind of the plan. He denounced the conspirators in the Senate, Catiline being present, and on the day of the election he had his own armed bands to keep order in the Field of Mars. Insurrection broke out in Etruria, but by Cicero's vigilance the simultaneous rising in the city failed. The general levy was called out, Catiline was presently forced to show his hand and flee from Rome, after failing to murder Cicero, and the insurrection became a miniature civil war. The chief conspirators in the city were arrested, and in the beginning of the new year Catiline himself was slain in a desperate fight in the Apennine passes, and the crisis was over. The Roman accomplices were by order of the Senate strangled in prison, and the consul who had saved the state was attended to his house by shouting crowds, and hailed by Cato and Catulus as *pater patriae*.

Cicero was for the moment the most popular man in Rome, for even the mob had been scared by the orgy of blood and ruin involved in Catiline's success. He deserved the plaudits which he won, for he had made no mistakes; his secret service was perfect; he gave Catiline the necessary rope to hang himself; he had the nerve not to act prematurely, and when the moment came he struck hard. The only criticism concerns the scene in the Senate, when the summary execution was ordered of the Roman accomplices. Clearly Cicero would have been justified in putting these men to death as an administrative act on his own authority; but the doubt arose when the Senate was asked to constitute itself a court of law, and pronounce sentence without trial on men who had not been taken in armed rebellion, but were only suspects.

Caesar was in a position of peculiar difficulty. He could not assent to the proposal for summary execution without stultifying all his previous career, and notably the action he had taken a few weeks earlier in the case of Rabirius. At the same time there was no moral doubt of their guilt, the crisis was urgent, with Catiline in arms beyond the walls, and to plead for leniency in the then state of popular feeling would have been almost to avow himself a sympathiser. As it was, he all but came by his death from the swords of the younger hot-bloods. In his speech, of which Sallust has preserved a full report, he pled for a sober judgement. It was

unconstitutional to put a citizen to death without trial, and might
be a fatal precedent. He showed that he had no confidence in the
use of the senatorial prerogative, even if justified by law, which it
was not; and he urged that, instead, the accused should be
imprisoned for life in certain Italian towns, which would effect the
practical purpose of keeping them out of mischief, and would not
be in the technical sense a 'capital' sentence. The speech,
embarrassed as it was, influenced opinion, and Cicero was almost
half-hearted in his reply. But Cato, the tribune-elect, clinched the
matter by arguing vehemently for the death penalty as an
administrative act – that abrogation of formal law in the face of
arms for which Marius had long ago provided the classic
formula.

After Catiline's death the excitement abated, and Caesar's
embarrassment was soon forgotten, the more so as Cicero let it be
known that some of the secret evidence about the plot had been
provided by Caesar himself. In the year 62 he was praetor, but we
do not know in what court he presided. His main interest was in
the intentions of Pompey, who, with the garlands of many
conquests about him, was waiting on the Aegean shore for the
proper moment to return, and had sent on ahead an emissary,
Metellus, to spy out the land. The Catiline affair had brought the
Optimates and the Populares closer together, the Senate was
making eyes at the mob, and on Cato's proposal the full corn
doles were restored. This must at all costs be prevented, and to
Caesar it seemed that Pompey might be made the wedge to split
the unnatural alliance. He proposed, therefore, that old Catulus
should be called to account for his expenditure on the new
Capitoline temple, that Pompey should complete it, and that the
inscription should bear Pompey's name. Caesar was thus beforehand
in offering oblation to the returning sun, an oblation which
annoyed the Senate, gave pleasure to Pompey, and cost himself
and his party nothing.

But the chief event of the year befell in his own family circle. In
December in his official residence there was celebrated according

to custom the annual rite of the Bona Dea, the goddess of fertility, to which only women were admitted. A young aristocrat, Clodius, brother of Catullus' 'Lesbia of the burning eyes,' had an intrigue with Pompeia, and managed to be present disguised as a music-girl. He was detected by Aurelia, who was suspicious of Pompeia, and Rome was agitated by a scandal of the first importance. Early in the new year Clodius was put on his trial for sacrilege, and Cicero, shocked to the core, was one of his chief prosecutors, thereby incurring his undying hate. The accused was acquitted owing to lavish bribery, and also, it would appear, because Caesar, the man chiefly concerned, did not press the charge. Caesar had indeed divorced Pompeia on the ground that his wife should be above even being suspected, but when called to give evidence he denied any personal knowledge of the facts. Perhaps he felt that scandalised virtue was scarcely the attitude for one on whose account Pompey had just put away his wife. Also he was not prepared to antagonise Clodius overmuch, for this strange degenerate was revealing remarkable qualities of mob leadership. He was already the chief gangster in Rome, and might be useful to one whose power over the mob was a prime political asset.

In the beginning of the year 61 Pompey landed at Brundisium, and Rome waited with anxiety for his next step. He had the chance, if he wished, to grasp the supreme power, a greater power than Sulla had ever held, for in the previous decade the fabric of the republic had rapidly disintegrated. But Pompey had no such ambition; if he had seized the autocracy, he would not have known what to do with it. To Cicero's delight he dismissed his legions and came to Rome as a private citizen; though, let it be remembered, this disbandment was rather a matter of form than of substance, for he had so loaded his veterans with bounties in his eastern campaign that he believed that he could recall them at will to his standard. He was ambitious only of personal glory, and had no far-seeing designs, his mind was not prescient or speculative, and there was a strong vein of laziness in his composition. Far more than to the reality of power he looked forward to the magnificent spectacle of his two days' triumph, when the riches of the East should be displayed before Roman eyes, and at the end, with the right Roman gesture, the new Alexander should put off his armour and return modestly like a second Cincinnatus to his home.

Pompey had been absent for five years, and he now stumbled upon a political witches' sabbath, which he was competent neither to direct nor to understand. The shouting in the streets was scarcely over before the aureole of glory deserted him. He was angry with the Senate, which had behaved cavalierly to his emissary Metellus, and had shown itself strangely unwilling to ratify his eastern settlement. His first speech was a frigid performance, which pleased, said Cicero, neither poverty nor rascaldom, nor capital, nor honesty. The Populares had treated him better, witness Caesar's action about the Capitoline temple, and he inclined towards them. Caesar was content. He might safely leave Pompey to his agents to manage, and he departed with an easy mind as propraetor to his province of Farther Spain.

The bulk of the year 61 and the early part of 60 were spent by Caesar in Andalusia and Portugal. Of his work there we know little. He fought his first little war as a commander-in-chief, a campaign against the hill tribes of Portugal and Galicia. On the civil side he dealt with the eternal problem of debt, and incidentally he himself became solvent again. He had owed something over a quarter of a million, and the bankers would have prevented him leaving Rome had not Crassus come to his aid. Now from the miserable system of confiscations and fees and the sale of captives, which was a governor's perquisite, he enriched his legions and cleared his own feet. In June 60 he was back in Rome, a candidate for the consulship.

His agents had well prepared the ground. His colleague on the popular side was one Lucceius, a rich dilettante whose function was merely to pay the expenses. He had been voted a triumph for his Spanish war, but the Senate declined to permit him to stand for the consulship without a personal canvass, a dispensation which it was within its power to make. Caesar, who never let vanity stand in the way of ambition, at once gave up his triumph, laid down his *imperium,* and entered the city. His first business was to complete that reconciliation of Pompey and Crassus at which his agents had been busily working. It was not difficult, since Pompey was at variance with the Senate, who had refused among other things to allot Italian lands to his veterans, and the Equites were furious because Cato – for what seem to have been excellent reasons – had prevented a reduction of their tender for the Asian taxes. With such support Caesar's election was certain, but his colleague was not Lucceius but Bibulus, the stiffest of senatorians.

The year 60 saw a greater event than Caesar's election, for it witnessed the first alliance of dynasts. This was wholly Caesar's doing. He was now at the difficult stage in a career when a man passes from the position of party chief to that of first citizen. To his clear eyes it seemed that in Rome there were three powers. There was the mob, which was his special asset, brilliantly organised through the street clubs and caucuses by ruffians of genius like Clodius. It was a power, but he had no respect for it; when he began it was the only weapon which lay to his hand, and he had made the most of it; but he loved the degraded business of personal canvassing and mob cajolery as little as did Cato himself. In the second place there were the capitalists, of whom Crassus was the patron and Cicero the somewhat dubious voice. Politics in Rome were an expensive game, and a leader must have a treasury. Last and most important, there was the army, and this meant Pompey, for that modest Roman was not only a successful general but could at will summon back to his side many legions.

Hitherto Caesar had played the game of demagogy with immense skill and as little principle as other people. But now the governance of Rome was falling into his hand, and he must prepare to accept it. There must be some promise of continuity in a reforming administration, and for this purpose there must be a coalition of all the elements which were not, like the senatorian reactionaries, altogether hostile to change. He believed honestly that he could work with both Pompey and Crassus, for their interests did not conflict with his; they wanted especially pomp, precedence, and spectacular honours, for which he himself cared not at all. How sincere Caesar was in his desire to build up a working coalition, a practical *concordia ordinum*, is shown by his attempt to enlist Cicero's support. But Cicero since his consulship had come to regard himself as the special guardian of the ancient constitution, and he suspected the orthodoxy of his boyhood's friend.

CHAPTER 5

The First Consulship

There is no warrant for believing that Caesar, when in 59 he entered upon his first consulship, had in his mind any far-reaching policy for the remaking of Rome. Hitherto he had been exercising his talents in a squalid game, building up a half-ruined party, climbing step by step the political ladder, using without much scruple whatever methods seemed to him the speediest and the best. He had not stopped to think about an ultimate goal, believing, with Cromwell, that no man goes so far as he who does not know where he is going. Now that he had reached the battlements he was still without a distant prospect. He had the consulship before him, and after that a province, and he was content to wait upon what they might bring forth. But he was already conscious of his supreme talents, conscious that he was far abler not only than his old colleagues of the half-world but than the gilded Crassus and the resplendent Pompey. He had discovered in himself the power of the administrator for putting crooked things straight and making difficult adjustments, and he desired an ampler opportunity of exercising that power. He believed, too, that he had a gift for war and for the creation of armies, and, knowing the weight of the sword in the balance, he was determined upon the enlargement of that gift. He was dimly aware that a great crisis was imminent which would decide the destiny of Rome, and he braced himself to meet it, though he could not forecast its form. Pompey and Crassus desired to be great figures, Caesar to do great deeds. The difference lay in what St Paul calls 'the substance of things hoped for,' the ultimate orientation of the spirit.

His first task was to strengthen his ties with Pompey and Crassus. To the former he gave in marriage his adored daughter Julia – a dynastic match, which seemed to Cicero to mean the end of the republic. He settled Pompey's veterans on the land, and ratified Pompey's eastern arrangements. Following the precedent of 71 and the Gabinio-Manilian laws, he was granted an extraordinary command for five years after the close of his consulship. The Senate would have given him as his proconsular province the management of the Italian roads and forests, but this farcical proposal was rejected, and by decrees of the Assembly he was given Cisalpine and Transalpine Gaul and Illyria with four legions. In his absence Pompey would keep an eye on Italy and Rome, and for the year 58 two safe men were elected consuls, the Pompeian Gabinius and Lucius Piso, who was Caesar's father-in-law. Crassus got nothing except a reduction in the contract for the Asian taxes, but he was encouraged to hope for a second consulship and a military command, and at the moment he was wholly under Caesar's spell.

Caesar attempted at first to work with the Senate, and treated it with studied courtesy. What he asked was in the circumstances not unreasonable, and he began by introducing all his measures in the orthodox way. He made some small reforms. If the Senate was to be of any value it must be made to face its responsibilities and be open to intelligent criticism, so he arranged for an official *Hansard,* and the regular publication of its debates. He was a pioneer also in popular journalism, for he ordered the magistrates to have a summary of important news inscribed on white-washed walls in various parts of the city. Then he entered upon his main legislative programme. Apart from the bills necessary to ratify his bargain with Pompey and Crassus, his chief measures were his agrarian laws and his attempt to reform provincial administration. The first flung open the rich district of Campania to settlement and provided from the treasury, now swollen with the proceeds of Pompey's conquests, money to buy further land. The second measure, the famous Lex Julia Repetundarum, stiffened the penalties for provincial extortion, and made every member of a governor's staff equally liable with the governor himself. It provided for copies of the governor's accounts being left for inspection in the province as well as forwarded to the Roman treasury, and it prohibited specifically what was already prohibited by the common law, the leading of an army beyond the province and the making of war without the mandate of Senate and people – a provision doubtless inserted to comfort tender conservative consciences.

But the Senate would have none of these measures or accept anything from Caesar. Cato tried to talk them out and had to be placed under arrest. Bibulus, the other consul, endeavoured to block them by declaring the auspices unfavourable. Caesar had no other course before him except to appeal to the Assembly and carry them by plebiscite. This was easily arranged. A tribune who attempted to veto the proceedings was brushed aside, and Bibulus was left in solitary grandeur to watch the skies. If the Senate chose to make government impossible it would be side-tracked at the cost of any informality, since the business of the state must be carried on.

But the vital event of the year was the determination of Caesar's proconsular province. Pompey had shown no jealousy of the five years' extraordinary command, for he had no reason to believe in Caesar's military gifts, and Gaul was not likely in his eyes to be the theatre of a great campaign. It was poor and barbarous and outside the ken of the civilised world. But Caesar was content. He had a liking for the people of Cisalpine Gaul, which he had already visited, and he had long been an earnest advocate of the claim of the district north of the Po to the Roman citizenship. As for Gaul beyond the mountains there seemed to be a flickering there which might soon be a flame. He was not thinking of conquests like Pompey's, but of making for himself an army and of winning a name as a defender of Rome in the field, and it looked as if there might soon be an opportunity there. Diviciacus the Aeduan chief had been in Rome two years before, and the Aedui had been specially marked for Rome's protection in their strife with the Burgundian Sequani. Now there seemed to be one of those strange stirrings, familiar in the Celtic world, among a Gallic tribe, the Helvetii, in the Swiss lowlands, who threatened to invade the Aeduan lands. Also the German Ariovistus, king of the Suebi, was a perpetual menace to Gaul. He had offered Rome his friendship, and, in order to gain time, the Senate had accepted him as an ally, but every one knew that the truce was hollow and that he was only waiting his chance to swoop westward on the Province of the Narbonne. North of the Alps there was no lack of tinder for the inevitable spark.

Caesar, sick of the wrangling in the Senate and Forum, full of the pioneer's passion for new lands, and eager for a life of action, had one task to accomplish before he set his face to the wilds. He must make easy the work of Pompey and Crassus by getting rid of the chief mischief-makers. Cato, on account of his surpassing virtue, was solemnly entrusted by plebiscite with a special mission to arrange the affairs of Cyprus, and departed unwillingly, taking with him a bookish nephew, one Marcus Brutus. Cicero was a more difficult case. For him Caesar had a sincere affection; he had tried to induce him to join the triumvirate; and, when he failed, he had proposed to take him with him on his staff to Gaul, an offer which an ex-consul and the leader of the bar could scarcely accept. But he must at all costs be got out of Rome, and Caesar's jackal, Clodius, was used for the purpose. Clodius, after getting himself adopted into a plebeian family, was elected tribune for the year 58, and his first act was to bring a bill before the Assembly punishing with exile anyone who had condemned a Roman citizen to death without an appeal to the people – a measure directly

39

aimed at Cicero. That honest man was filled with disquiet, for by means of his clubs and his gangsters Clodius was certain to carry his measure. From Crassus he could expect nothing, and his senatorian friends were apathetic or powerless. Pompey, when Cicero flung himself at his feet, referred him to Caesar. Caesar repeated his offer of a post on his staff, but did nothing more. He would not call off his hound if Cicero could not be induced to leave Rome by gentler means. So he kept his legions near the walls till the end of March, and not till he heard that the disconsolate philosopher had turned his melancholy steps towards Brundisium did he hurry north along the Flaminian Way.

CHAPTER 6

The Conquest of Gaul

He had need for haste, for out of Gaul had come ominous news. The Helvetii were moving; in a few days they would assemble opposite Geneva, a multitude nearly four hundred thousand strong, with the purpose of crossing the Rhone, sweeping through the Roman Province, and seizing lands in the west in the vale of the Charente, where the cornfields of the Province would be at their mercy. Travelling twenty miles a day Caesar crossed the Alps, and in a week was at Geneva. It was to be nine years before he trod his native soil again.

Gaul at the time contained three great tribal conglomerations. In the south-west the Aquitani held the country between the Garonne and the Pyrenees; the Celtae occupied the Mediterranean and Atlantic seaboards, the lowlands of Switzerland and the upper Rhine, and the uplands of central France; while in the north and north-east, the Belgae ruled from the Aisne to the Channel, and from the Seine to the Rhine. The Province itself and some parts of the interior had acquired a tincture of Roman civilisation, but elsewhere the Gauls were a primitive people, farmers and pastoralists and hunters, hardy and frugal, a big-boned, loose-limbed folk with flaxen hair and a ruddy colour, fine horsemen and stout foot-soldiers. Their mode of government varied between monarchy, oligarchy, and a rudimentary democracy, but their chief loyalty was tribal. A tribe might be a member of a confederacy, but it cherished a fierce individuality and independence.

To Rome, though she had fought its people more than once, Gaul was largely an unknown land, and being unknown it was feared. At any hour out of those northern swamps and forests might come a new torrent which no second Marius could stem. Gaul and Parthia were the danger-points of the Roman frontier. Moreover Ariovistus and his Germans, though they were for the moment quiescent, were an imminent thunder-cloud. Caesar realised that Gaul was the coming storm-centre, and that his proconsulship might begin with petty wars, but was certain to develop problems of the first gravity. He desired to make an army which would be his chief weapon in the uncertainties of the future; he desired the same kind of prestige as Pompey had won; he was as confident as Napoleon in his star, and he was conscious of his supereminent talents. But he was above all things an opportunist and was content to let his policy be shaped by events. His first duty was the defence of Italy. He knew little of the land he was bound for, and realised that he must be explorer as well as soldier; the passages in his *Commentaries* where he describes the nature of the country and the habits of the people show how keen was his scientific interest. Above all he welcomed a life of action under the open sky, for his health was beginning to suffer from the stuffy *coulisses* of Roman politics, and he faced joyfully the unplumbed chances of the years before him, for he had never feared the unknown.

He was beginning his serious military career at the age of forty-four, much the same age as Cromwell's when he took the field. But every Roman had a smattering of military knowledge, the technique of war was still elementary, and for twenty years Caesar had been practised in commanding and influencing men. He already possessed that eye for country, that coolness in a crisis, and that speed and boldness in decision which no staff college can give. The Roman army, since the Marian reforms, was a more effective fighting force. Its strength lay in its non-commissioned officers, in its iron discipline and marching powers, in its superior equipment in the way of small arms and artillery, and in its superb auxiliary services, for the Roman soldier was the best trench-digger and bridge-builder in the world. Caesar had slingers from the Balearic Isles, and archers from Numidia and Crete, and cavalry from Spain, but he intended to recruit most of his horse in Gaul itself. He began with the three legions in Cisalpine Gaul, where he presently enrolled two more, and one, the famous Tenth, in the Province* – a force of some 20,000 men. He enlisted no infantry beyond the Alps, and all his conquering legions were drawn from the mixed population of Piedmont and the Lombard plain. They were a stocky type, a foot shorter than the average Gaul, but stalwart in nerve, muscle, and discipline.

The eight years of the Gallic campaigns will repay the attentive study of all who are interested in the art of war. Here we can only glance at the main movements. The first task was the migrating Helvetii. They hoped to cross the Rhone below Geneva and march through Savoy, but Caesar destroyed the existing bridge, fortified the left bank of the river, and compelled them to try the passes of the Jura. With the help of the Aeduan chief Dumnorix, the rival of Diviciacus, they had secured an unimpeded passage through the territory of the Sequani. While their long train was winding among the mountains, Caesar hurried back to Cisalpine Gaul for his new legions, recrossed the Alps by way of Mont Genèvre, hastened through Dauphiny, and came up with the Helvetii as they were crossing the Saone. There he cut off their rearguard, and headed them north into the Burgundian plain. He found himself in difficulty over supplies, and Dumnorix, who commanded his Aeduan cavalry, was not to be trusted. After fifteen days' pursuit he forced the Helvetii to give battle near the Aeduan capital Bibracte (Mont Beuvray, near Autun), and after a

---

* Caesar was probably the first man to number his legions, thereby giving them identity and a continuity of tradition.

long and desperate day completely routed them. He was fighting against odds of two to one, and his troops were still untempered. The remnant of the Helvetii were sent back to their old home, and he turned to the graver menace of Ariovistus.

Caesar's lightning speed, which had routed the Helvetii, proved also the undoing of the German chieftain. Ariovistus was then in upper Alsace. The victory of Bibracte had swung over the doubting Gallic tribes to the Roman side, and they were eager to fling off the superiority which he had imposed on them. Caesar began with diplomacy, asking only that further German immigration west of the Rhine should cease, but he received a haughty reply, and the news that a fresh army of Suebi was mustering on the east bank of the river. He delayed no longer, but marched straight for Vesontio (Besançon), the capital of the Sequani, which he made his base. He had some trouble with his troops, especially with the unwarlike military tribunes, who were awed by the legendary prowess of the Germans, and he restored confidence by one of those speeches which he knew how to direct straight to men's hearts. 'If no one else follows me,' he said, 'I go on with the Tenth legion alone, and I make it my bodyguard.'

He marched through the Gap of Belfort and found Ariovistus on the Rhine near Mülhausen. Some days were wasted in idle negotiations, during which the treachery of the Germans became clear. Then Ariovistus marched his army westward along the foothills of the Vosges, with the obvious intention of cutting off the Roman line of supply. Six days later Caesar forced him to give battle, by threatening him in flank and rear. The engagement of September 18th was fought on the plan of Austerlitz, the weak Roman right forming a hinge on which the rest of the army swung to break the enemy's right and centre. Caesar's left was for some time in a critical position, and was saved by young Publius Crassus, the son of Marcus, the commander of the cavalry, who flung in his reserves at the critical moment. The enemy was cut to pieces, Ariovistus fled across the Rhine, and for several centuries the German overflooding of Gaul was stayed.

In the autumn of 58 Caesar withdrew his troops into winter quarters in the country of the Sequani, and, leaving Titus Labienus in command, returned to Cisalpine Gaul. He had technically broken the provision of his own Julian law by leading his army beyond his province, and to winter it outside Roman territory was a still more daring innovation. His formal justification was that he had the express instructions of the Senate to protect the Aedui, and that this was the only way of doing it; his real defence was the compulsion of facts. He had come to realise the weakness of Gaul, split up among a hundred jealous tribes; if he could bring it under Roman sway he would not only make the frontier secure, but would add to the empire a race which he greatly admired, and which, he believed, would be an invaluable possession for the future. His dream was shaping itself of a new kind of empire, the strength of which would lie not in its wealth and its relics of an older civilisation but in the quality of its people. In the free air of the north he felt his body invigorated and his mind clarified, and he was now convinced beyond a peradventure of his genius for war. That winter he perfected his plans for the conquest of all Gaul.

In the spring of 57 he set out on his great errand. Central and southern Gaul were his, but the fierce people of the north, the Belgae, were unconquered, and he had word that they were mustering to drive out the Romans. He had enrolled two new legions in Lombardy, which gave him a total of eight – perhaps 40,000 men. From Besançon he marched into Champagne, where he made the Remi, who dwelt around Rheims and Châlons, a Roman nucleus like the Aedui further south. He found two of the chief Belgic tribes, the Suessiones (dwelling around Soissons) and the Bellovaci (around Beauvais), drawn up on the heights north of the Aisne. He crossed the river in the neighbourhood of Berry-au-bac, and built an entrenched camp as his advanced base. The enemy found this position impregnable, and, being in difficulties about supplies, began to retreat. They were pursued by Labienus and the cavalry, who punished them severely. Caesar swung westward and took order with the Bellovaci and the Suessiones, capturing the chief town of the latter. Then he marched north against the heart of the Belgic confederacy, the strong nation of the Nervii, who dwelt in the woody flats along the Scheldt and the Sambre, that land which was destined to be the cockpit of later history. Here he encountered an enemy worthy of his steel. The Nervii at some point between Charleroi and Namur surprised the Romans, and there ensued a soldier's battle like Malplaquet, fought not very far from the scene of Marlborough's victory. Caesar himself was compelled to fight in the ranks to maintain the spirit of his troops, till the arrival of his brigade of Guards, the Tenth legion, turned the tide. The Nervii were all but annihilated, the Belgic confederacy was dissolved, and the campaign was won. They were of all the enemies he encountered the one whom he most admired, and his sober prose kindles almost to a sober poetry when he describes their unavailing courage.

The news of this decisive battle created a profound sensation in Rome. The Senate, after Caesar's despatch had been read, decreed a public thanksgiving of fifteen days – Pompey had only had ten days for Mithridates. Affairs in the capital were in a curious position. Clodius, Caesar's party manager, had kept the Populares active by every kind of fantastic law and criminal outrage. But popular feeling was turning against that demagogue, and Caesar was beginning to see the need for calling off his hound. He was always prepared to make use of blackguards; he did not like the pious rogue and preferred his ruffians to be naked and unashamed; but he never permitted the rascality of an agent to go beyond the bounds of policy. He made no objection to the recall of Cicero as a concession to the respectable classes, and that homesick exile was given a great popular reception when he returned in September. Pompey had found a jackal of his own, the tribune Milo, who was ready to stand up to Clodius, and it was very necessary to keep Pompey in good humour. Cicero, grateful to his laggard patron, carried a proposal in the Senate to give Pompey for five years complete control of the Roman corn supply and the supervision of all ports and markets in the empire, and Caesar's agents readily agreed. Something had to be done for Pompey to prevent him growing jealous of the repute which Caesar was winning so fast. But Pompey was not satisfied. He saw that he was now only a figure-head; he wanted real power once more, and that meant an army and an independent command; and he did not see how he could get it without alienating those conservatives who were now sedulously cultivating him, and who were whispering in his ear that he was the only hope of the republic.

In the year 56 the Gallic operations languished. Caesar paid a visit to his other province of Illyria, leaving it to his lieutenants to deal with the Aquitani in the south-west, and the maritime tribes of the Atlantic coast. Labienus on the Moselle kept an eye on the Germans, and Publius Crassus had a short and brilliant campaign against the Aquitani. But the Veneti in southern Brittany gave more trouble, and a fleet had to be collected and partly built on the Loire, with which Decimus Brutus, during a long summer's day while the legions looked on from the mainland cliffs, won one of the most curious naval battles in history. Caesar behaved to the conquered tribes with what may seem extreme brutality, for he put the chiefs to death and sold the rest of the males as slaves. His defence, which he states frankly, was that they had broken the law as to the inviolability of envoys, and that, in order to protect his future supplies, it was necessary to read them a sharp lesson. Then he turned east along the Channel coast and subdued the Morini and the Menapii, Belgic tribes who had been allies of the Veneti and who dwelt in the Pas de Calais and Flanders. From the shore he saw the distant cliffs of the 'white land,' and his explorer's interest was awakened in the strange island of the north from which the secret religion of the Gauls drew its inspiration.

If in that year the Gallic war had few notable incidents, it was otherwise with the political game in Rome. Authority seemed to have gone both from the senatorian conservatives and from the great capitalists, and a younger set, without morals or policy, people like Mark Antony and Curio and Caelius, were casting their lines in the troubled waters. Catullus, the genius of the decadence, was abusing Pompey and Caesar in the lofty conservative vein which is only possible for an aspiring scion of the middle classes. Pompey was finding his life intolerable from the mischievous pranks of Clodius on the one side and the pedantic denunciations of Cato on the other. Caesar, watching the political game from north of the Po, saw that things were nearing a crisis, and that that crisis must be averted if he was to complete his work in Gaul. Domitius Ahenobarbus, a rich and stubborn senatorian, was candidate for next year's consulship, and he made no secret of his intention to demand Caesar's recall. Cicero, too, in the beginning of April proposed in the Senate that Caesar's Campanian land policy should be put down for discussion in the following month. Unless immediate action were taken the arrangement of 59 would crumble.

Caesar acted promptly. He invited Pompey and Crassus to meet him in the middle of April at Luca (Lucca) in the extreme south of his province. Thither they duly came, attended by a host of senators and political aspirants, and there the triumvirate was re-established, since the three, if they were but agreed, were omnipotent. Caesar offered liberal terms – far too liberal if he had consulted his own interests; but he was eager to have the matter settled and to get on with his work in the north, he liked Pompey, and he was determined to do nothing to hurt his beloved Julia. Pompey and Crassus were to be next year's consuls, and thereafter to have the governorships of Spain and Syria respectively for a term of five years. Pompey might stay in Rome and administer Spain by lieutenants, but Crassus was to be permitted to realise the dream of his life and lead from his province an army to the conquest of Parthia. Caesar was to be confirmed in his proconsulship of Gaul for a second space of five years – that is to the beginning of 49.

The terms were gladly and gratefully accepted, for they relieved Pompey from an impossible position and they gave Crassus all that he had ever dreamed. Somehow Clodius was put on the leash, and Cicero's support was not long in doubt. In June in the Senate the latter made one of the best of all his speeches in defence of the Luca arrangements, and he praised Caesar's Gallic exploits with insight and eloquence. The conquest of Gaul, he said, was not the mere annexation of a province, but the dispersion of the one menace to the empire. The Alps had been piled by Heaven as a rampart for Italy, but now they might sink to earth, since Italy had nothing to fear. There is something more in the speech than forensic rhetoric; there is a real admiration for Caesar's greatness. Cicero had been snubbed and ignored by arrogant senatorians and left in the lurch by Pompey, and he turned to his boyhood's friend who had always treated him kindly. 'Since those who have no power,' he wrote to Atticus, 'will have none of my love, let me take care that those who have the power shall love me.' Caesar met him halfway. He took his brother Quintus as one of his general officers, corresponded with him regularly on literary matters, read and praised his bad verses, and lent him money. For the moment Cicero was an ardent Caesarian, convinced, as he said, by his judgement, his sense of duty and the promptings of his heart. 'I burn with love for him.'

The Luca conference gave Rome a brief interlude of peace. In the year 55, Caesar to complete his conquests, had to look to the Rhine frontier. Two powerful German tribes, the Usipetes and the Tencteri, had been forced by the Suebi to cross to the west bank of the river, and were now a dangerous element on the edge of Gaul, since these bold mercenaries were being courted by all the Gallic malcontents. He determined to crush this coalition so sternly that it would never again revive. He marched against the newcomers and ordered them back. They prevaricated and argued, and some of their horse made a treacherous attack on a body of Roman cavalry; with this as his justification Caesar detained their chiefs, who had come to confer, and launched his legions against the leaderless hordes; there was a great massacre and few recrossed the Rhine. It is a ghastly tale, the ugliest episode of the Gallic wars, and it was unsparingly condemned in the Senate by Cato and by more reasonable men than Cato. But Caesar, merciful both by temperament and policy, seems to have had no doubt about the justice of his action. The German peril was not to be trifled with, and the German demand for westward expansion could only be answered 'by sharp pens and bloody ink.' Then he proceeded to deal with the Sugambri, a tribe east of the Rhine; they had been giving trouble to the Ubii, who were allies of Rome. His purpose was to teach the powerful Suebi that if they threatened Gaul he could assuredly threaten Germany. He bridged the Rhine at a point between Coblenz and Andernach, a marvellous feat of engineering, and remained eighteen days on German soil, while the Sugambri fled to the dark forests of the interior.

The rest of the summer was occupied with the first expedition to Britain. On August 26th he sailed from Portus Itius (between Calais and Boulogne, perhaps Wissant), and found himself early next morning off the coast west of Dover. The tide carried him down channel, and the landing was made on the low shores of Romney marsh. It was not seriously opposed, but the unfamiliar tides played havoc with his ships. While they were being repaired, an attack of the natives was beaten off and the local tribes sued for peace. After taking hostages he put to sea again, and reached Gaul in safety. It had been only a reconnaissance, but the second expedition was a more serious affair. All winter ships were being built, and on the 20th day of the following July – after some trouble with his Gallic horse, in which the Aeduan Dumnorix was killed – Caesar sailed again, with five legions and a considerable body of cavalry. He landed on the beach at Deal, entrenched a camp, and marched into the interior. He found himself opposed by a strange people, who tattooed their bodies with a blue dye, and were uncommonly skilful in their use of war chariots. Their king was one Cassivelaunus (Cadwallon), whose capital was near St Albans. Caesar crossed the Thames, and after some desultory fighting forced the king to submit. But it was impossible to winter his legions there, and the conquest of the country was clearly a large undertaking with little hope of profit. After taking the usual hostages and fixing a tribute which was certainly never paid, Caesar returned to Deal and recrossed the Channel. His purpose had been partly scientific – to see for himself a mysterious land and people; partly military, for to Britain could be traced some of the threads of Gallic unrest; and largely political. The crossing of the Channel, like the bridging of the Rhine, was the kind of feat that fired the imagination of Rome, and gave to its performer a mystic aura of invincibility.

When he returned from Britain in the autumn of 54, Caesar may well have regarded the conquest of Gaul as a thing accomplished. He had carried the Roman arms to every corner of the land, and even beyond the Rhine and the narrow seas. He had been merciless when mercy seemed to him short-sighted, as in the case of the Veneti and the German invaders, but his general policy had been one of conciliation. He had made partisans of many of the Gallic leaders, and he had provided a profession for warlike youth by forming a new Fifth legion, the 'Lark,' entirely from Gauls. As for the situation in Rome, he was spending the immense sums he had won from his proconsul's perquisites in lending money to needy citizens and in erecting superb public buildings as gifts to the people. Pompey and Crassus were attached to him by strong ties of self-interest, and Cicero had become a friend and a panegyrist instead of a critic. He looked forward to five years more in Gaul in which he could make the province a loyal daughter of Rome, and then to a second consulship when he could realise the ideas which were slowly growing up in his mind as to the future shaping of the empire.

These happy forecasts were rudely shattered. He had still to face the inevitable reaction. During three desperate years he had to reconquer Gaul, and then find himself forced unwillingly to conquer the world.

CHAPTER 7

The Revolt of Gaul

The trouble began during the winter of 54, and, as was to be expected, among the Belgae. That winter Caesar tarried in the north, for the harvest had been bad and supplies were difficult, and he was compelled to distribute his army over a wide extent of country. His own headquarters were at Amiens; one legion, under Fabius, was among the Morini north of the Scheldt, one under Quintus Cicero among the Nervii at Charleroi, and one under Labienus among the Treveri near Sedan. One, consisting of Gallic recruits but strengthened by five veteran cohorts, was among the Eburones at Aduatuca, in the neighbourhood of Liège. Around him in the Amiens and Beauvais district he had three under Trebonius, Plancus, and the quaestor Marcus Crassus, whose younger brother Publius had now gone to Syria with his father.

The winter had scarcely begun and Caesar was still at Amiens when the plot which had been maturing during his absence in Britain revealed itself at Aduatuca. In command there were two officers, Sabinus and Aurunculeius Cotta, of whom the former was the senior. Ambiorix, the chief of the Eburones, attacked the entrenched camp, and, being beaten off, asked for a parley. Protesting that he had been driven against his desire into hostilities, he told a circumstantial tale of how all Gaul, with German support, was rising against the Romans, and urged the commanders to join hands at once with Caesar and Labienus, guaranteeing that they would not be attacked on the road. Caesar was a hundred and fifty miles off, and the nearest legion, Quintus Cicero's at Charleroi, was forty-five miles away. Sabinus, with only 6000 men, most of them half-trained, fell into the trap. He set out at dawn, and found himself surrounded by the enemy. He and Cotta were slain, and a mere handful escaped to Labienus.

Ambiorix, swollen with victory, now persuaded the Nervii to attack Quintus Cicero. Cicero was in bad health, and the attack came as a complete surprise to him, but he was of different metal from Sabinus. He sent messengers to Caesar to report the situation, beat off the assault, and, in response to Ambiorix's overtures, declared that Romans made no terms with an enemy in arms. Then began a desperate siege. All the stores and baggage were burned by the enemy's fireballs, and presently nine men out of ten of the little force were dead or wounded. Meantime no word came from Caesar, and it was doubtful if any had reached him, for messenger after messenger was caught by the enemy and tortured to death under the Romans' eyes.

But one got through. At last a javelin was found stuck in one of the towers, with a message in Greek, 'Be of good courage, help is at hand'; it had been flung by one of Caesar's Gallic horsemen. Very soon the besieged saw clouds of smoke on the horizon, and knew that the Nervii villages were burning, and that Caesar was near. When the solitary messenger from Cicero reached Amiens, Caesar at once sent word to Crassus to come and take his place, to Fabius to join him on the road, and to Labienus to move to Cicero's aid if he could. Then by forced marches he covered the eighty miles to Charleroi. He had only two legions, for Labienus was himself in straits and could not join him. Ambiorix, with his 60,000 men, advanced to crush the 8000 of the relieving force, but Caesar refused to be drawn into a precipitate battle. He entrenched a small camp which was an invitation to the enemy's attack; the attack duly came, the Gauls were admitted almost inside the ramparts, and then like a thunderclap came the unexpected counterstroke, and Ambiorix's horde was driven panic-stricken into the marshes. Caesar did not pursue them, but marched on to Charleroi without the loss of a single man. There he congratulated Cicero and his gallant remnant on their new Thermopylae, and there he heard the tragic tale of Aduatuca. The news of the relief spread like wildfire, and Labienus was freed from the threats of Indutiomarus and the Treveri.

Caesar spent an anxious winter among his troops, with the legions of Quintus Cicero and Crassus concentrated round Amiens. He had many conferences with the Gallic chiefs, and from these it was clear that a new and dangerous spirit was abroad. The slaughter of the cohorts at Aduatuca had inflamed racial pride, and everywhere in the province there was a muttering of unrest. Labienus, indeed, held his own among the Treveri, and Indutiomarus was slain, but though the flame died down the ashes smouldered. Caesar raised two new legions in Cisalpine Gaul, and borrowed a third from Pompey, who had no need of troops, since he refused to go near his province of Spain. When the campaigning season opened in 53 he led punitive expeditions against malcontent tribes like the Nervii and the Menapii; crossed the Rhine again to overawe the Suebi, and made an example of the Eburones, though Ambiorix succeeded in escaping into the fastnesses of the Ardennes. In the autumn he quartered most of his legions further south in the neighbourhood of Sens and Langres, and returned to Cisalpine Gaul to keep an eye upon Rome.

He had no sooner crossed the Alps than revolution broke out, and a far more formidable enemy appeared than Ambiorix or Indutiomarus. The fiery cross was sent round, secret meetings were held everywhere, and a consciousness of nationality, a sense that now was the last chance for regaining their lost freedom, inspired even many of those Gauls who had appeared to be devotees of Rome. This popular movement for a time brought about unity among the fissiparous tribes, and it found its leader in Vercingetorix. He was a young Arvernian noble, whose father had once attempted to make himself king of Gaul. To ancestral prestige he added high military talent, and a character which both charmed and impressed all who met him. That winter he was busy among the villages of Auvergne, and his emissaries visited all the neighbouring tribes, till by the new year he had a vast mass of tinder waiting for the spark.

The spark came with an attack by the Cornutes upon the Roman commissaries at Orleans. Vercingetorix from his headquarters at Gergovia, the mountain town south-east of the Puy de Dôme, sent out his summons for revolt. He had a plan with which he believed he could conquer. He could dispose of great clouds of cavalry, and the Gallic horse, who had been the mounted arm of the Romans, had during the recent troubles melted away. He would never attack the unshakable legions, but he would cut off their supplies and with his cavalry shepherd them to starvation and disaster. Above all he would deprive them of Caesar's leading. A belt of revolution would prevent their commander-in-chief from reaching them on the upper Seine, and he believed that he was the match of Quintus Cicero and Labienus.

The news reached Caesar in early February in Cisalpine Gaul. The situation was desperate. Affairs in Rome urgently demanded his attention, for his party there seemed to be crumbling, but in Gaul it looked as if the labour of seven years had come to naught. The trouble now was not in the north and east, but in the centre and the south, which he thought had been finally pacified. The very Province itself was in danger. Of all the tribes he could count only on the Remi, the Lingones, and the Aedui, and he did not know how long he could be sure of the Aedui. He crossed the Alps without drawing rein, and in the Province his difficulties began. How was he to rejoin his legions? If he sent for them they would have to cut their way south without their general; if he tried to reach them he ran an imminent risk of capture. All the rebel country lay between him and his army.

The one hope lay in boldness, and his boldness was like a flame. He arranged for the defence of the Province, and then in deep snow raced through the passes of the Cevennes, which no man before had travelled in winter. He was carrying fire and sword over the Auvergne plateau when the enemy still thought of him as south of the Alps. Vercingetorix hastened to meet him, which was what Caesar desired. He had drawn the rebel army on a false scent. Leaving Decimus Brutus to hold it, he returned to Vienne on the Rhone, picked up some waiting cavalry, galloped up the Saone valley through the doubtful Aedui, and early in March joined his legions at Langres. While Vercingetorix was still entangled with Decimus Brutus, Caesar had concentrated ten legions in his rear at Agedincum on the Yonne. He had won the first round.

The events of the months that followed, the most hazardous and the most brilliant in Caesar's military career, must be briefly summarised. Vercingetorix was forced by public opinion to be false to his own wise strategic creed, and was compelled to defend the city of Avaricum (Bourges). He cut off Caesar's supplies and reduced his army to scarecrows, but the Roman fortitude did not weaken. Avaricum was carried by assault after four weeks' siege, and the fate of its people was a terrible warning. Then Vercingetorix flung himself into Gergovia with a large army, and Caesar sat down to a blockade – a difficult task, for Labienus was away on the Seine with four legions and the besiegers had only some 95,000 men. Moreover Caesar had to leave the siege to punish the Aedui, who were sending a large contingent to the enemy. He tried to take Gergovia by assault, and was repulsed with heavy loss – his first blunder and his first defeat. He could not induce Vercingetorix to give battle, and meantime his supplies were being systematically cut off by the Gallic horse. The Aedui were in open revolt, Labienus was in difficulties further north, and the Province was in dire danger. Caesar bowed to the compulsion of facts, raised the siege of Gergovia, and crossed the Loire into Aeduan territory. There he found supplies, effected a junction with Labienus, and received a contingent of German cavalry which he had sent for from the Ubii. He turned south-east into the country of the Sequani, his plan being apparently to secure there a base of operations which would enable him to defend the Province and keep open his communications with Italy, and from which he could begin again the conquest of Gaul.

Vercingetorix played into his hand. In a great assembly at Bibracte he had been made high chief of all Gaul, and his elevation seems to have weakened his caution. He attacked Caesar on the march, and was so roughly handled that he decided that he could not face the Romans in the field, so he flung himself into the mountain citadel of Alesia (Mont Auxois) above the little river Brenne, where he hoped to repeat the success of Gergovia. Around the hill Caesar drew elaborate siege-works and beat off all the sallies of the besieged. The messengers of Vercingetorix summoned aid from every corner of Gaul, the national spirit burned fiercely, and a relieving force of no less than a quarter of a million infantry and 8000 horse assembled. Caesar with his 50,000 foot and his German cavalry was now enclosed between Vercingetorix and the hordes of his new auxiliaries; the besieger had become also the besieged. The full tale of that miraculous longdrawn fight – the greatest of Caesar's battles and one of the greatest in history – must be read in Caesar's own narrative. In the end the relieving force was decisively beaten, Alesia surrendered, and the Gallic revolt was over.

Vercingetorix in defeat rose to heroic stature. He offered his life for his countrymen, for, as he said, he had been fighting for Gaul and not for himself; splendidly accoutred he appeared before Caesar, stripped off his arms and laid them silently at his feet. The victor for reasons of policy showed mercy to the broken Aedui and Arverni, but he had none for Vercingetorix. He was sent to Rome as a prisoner, six years later he adorned his conqueror's triumph, and then he was put to death in a dungeon of the Capitol. No Roman, not even Caesar, knew the meaning of chivalry. Of Vercingetorix we may say that he was the first, and not the least, of that succession of Celtic paladins to whom the freedom of their people has been a burning faith. He was the greatest soldier –

greater than Pompey – that Caesar ever faced in the field, and no lost cause could boast a nobler or more tragical hero.

At last Gaul was not only conquered but pacified, and never again did she seriously threaten Rome. Indeed she was destined to remain the last repository of the Roman tradition, and its mellow afterglow had not wholly gone from her skies when it was replaced by the dawn of the Renaissance. At this point in his chronicle Caesar lays down his pen. He wintered among the Aedui, and next year was engaged in small operations to consolidate his power. His main task now was to organise the new province, and, though it was probably not formally annexed to Rome till his dictatorship, he was already organising its government and assessing its tribute. He was also winning his way into the hearts of many of the leading Gauls, so that in the later crisis of his fortunes they stood unflinchingly by his side.

The campaigns in Gaul are Caesar's chief title to what has never been denied him, a place in the inner circle of the world's captains. He was in the first place a superb trainer of troops. He raised at least five new legions, and he so handled them that they soon ranked as veterans. Again, he was a great leader of men, having that rare gift of so diffusing his personality that every soldier felt himself under his watchful eye and a sharer in his friendship. Strategically he had an infallible eye for country, a geographical instinct as sure as Napoleon's. He had that power of simplification which belongs only to genius, and he never wasted his strength in divergent operations, but struck unerringly at the vital point. A desperate crisis only increased his coolness and the precision of his thought. He understood the minds of men, and played unerringly on the psychology of both his own soldiers and the enemy's; indeed he made the enemy do half his work for him; and he had a kind of boyish gusto which infected his troops with his own daring and speed. He had able marshals, like Labienus and Quintus Cicero and Publius Crassus, but he was always the controlling spirit. He was essentially humane – 'mitis clemensque natura,' Cicero wrote – but he was implacable when policy required it. Nor must it be forgotten that in his generalship, as in that of all great captains, there was a profound statesmanship. He never forgot that success in the field was only a means to an end, and that his purpose was not to defeat an army but to conquer and placate a nation.

CHAPTER 8

The Rubicon

The years of the revolt in Gaul saw the gradual breakdown of the Luca settlement and the dissolution of the triumvirate. While Caesar was fighting for his life against odds every despatch from Rome brought news of the worsening of his political prospects, and, adroit party chief as he was, he could not at that distance and in the midst of so many urgent tasks control successfully the party game. In the autumn of 54 Julia died, his only child and Pompey's wife, and she was soon followed by his mother, Aurelia. Julia's infant son did not long survive her, and so the family tie between the two dynasts was broken. Pompey was proving himself wholly unable to control the anarchy in the capital. 'We have lost,' Cicero wrote despairingly, 'not only the blood and sap, but even the outward hue and complexion of the commonwealth as it used to be.' That disillusioned man could only solace his enforced leisure by writing political philosophy in which he portrayed his ideal republic. His chief consolation was his friendship with Caesar, who found posts for every friend he recommended, and entrusted him with the spending of great sums on his new public buildings. For the moment he ranked with Oppius and Balbus as one of Caesar's agents.

Next year the triumvirate suffered a further shock, for Crassus perished in his Parthian campaign. The ambitions of the luckless millionaire ended miserably among the Mesopotamian sands, and his bloody head was flung on to the stage at the Parthian court, where a company of strolling players were performing the *Bacchae* of Euripides. The East had triumphed over the West, and the quaestor Gaius Cassius had much ado to lead the remnant of the beaten army back to Syria. On Crassus Caesar could always reckon, but Pompey alone was an easy mark for the intrigues of the Optimates, and he began to drift rapidly away from his ally. He refused Caesar's offer of the hand of his great-niece Octavia, and chose instead a daughter of Metellus Scipio, one of the most rigid of the senatorians. The year closed with a political pandemonium, in which it was impossible to hold the consular elections. Daily there was bloodshed in the streets, and Cicero was nearly killed on the Sacred Way.

In January 52 Clodius, the bravo of the Populares, was slain in a brawl on the Appian Way by Milo, the bravo of the Optimates and a recent candidate for the consulship. This brought matters to a head, for some kind of order must be restored. Pompey, on the motion of Bibulus and Cato, was made sole consul for the year; that is, a virtual dictator. He had now ranged himself definitely on the side of the Optimates, and that year saw the end of the triumvirate; for, though he still professed to be in alliance with Caesar, all his measures were cunningly directed against Caesar's interests, while Caesar, busy with the Gallic revolt, could reply only by providing feasts and shows for the populace. In the blackguard Clodius he had lost his most audacious and resourceful henchman. One of Pompey's laws provided that no consul or praetor could proceed to his province till five years after holding office. He approved a bill introduced by the tribunes and carried by plebiscite, permitting Caesar to stand for the consulship while absent from Rome, but this concession seemed to be abrogated by a further law which confirmed the old rule about a personal canvass. Caesar's proconsular office formally terminated on March

1, 49, but since he was entitled to his *imperium* until the arrival of his successor, it would really continue till the end of that year. Unless he were elected consul for 48 he would become a private citizen, and as such would certainly be impeached and probably killed; but he could not lay down his *imperium* without becoming a private person, and he could not retain it if he left his province; therefore he must be allowed to be a candidate while still with his army. Such had been the Luca arrangement, and now Pompey seemed to be trying to whittle it away. The plot against Caesar was revealing itself.

Next year, 51, Caesar, his task accomplished, published his *Commentaries* on the Gallic war. His purpose was twofold: to give a succinct soldierly narrative of the great struggle and to interest the Roman people in their new dominion; and to show that the campaign had been forced upon him by dire necessity and that he had only acted in accordance with the spirit of the constitution. The book was primarily an electioneering pamphlet, the most brilliant known to history. The consuls in this year, Sulpicius Rufus and Marcus Marcellus, were both senatorians; the first, one of the few attractive figures of the time, might be trusted to act fairly, but Marcellus was a violent partisan, and, like Cato, made no secret of his intention to have Caesar recalled. The cabal was now plain for all to see, and Pompey had gone over body and soul to the conservatives. One incident showed how the wind blew. Caesar had always maintained that the Transpadanes, the dwellers north of the Po, were Roman burgesses as of right, but a town-councillor of Novum Comum came to Rome, and Marcellus had him flogged (Pompey not objecting) for pretending to the Roman citizenship – a glaring insult to the proconsul of Gaul.

In the year 50 the plot spread fast. One consul, Aemilius Paullus, was a Caesarian, and all but one of the tribunes. One of the latter, Curio, now came to the front. He had been a bitter critic of Caesar in the past, but Caesar had won him over by paying his numerous debts, and he became his principal agent, more respectable than Clodius and more effective because less freakish. The nature of the attack had declared itself, and Caesar, back now in Cisalpine Gaul, could watch the various moves. His provincial command must in any case cease by January 1, 48. He had the right to expect that his successor would be one of the consuls for 49, who would only relieve him in 48, by which time he himself would be consul. He had also been given the right of standing for the consulship *in absentia*. But Pompey's law, enjoining an interval of five years between the consulship and a proconsulship, enabled the Senate to appoint to a province for 48 anyone of consular rank. Caesar therefore would be actually relieved of his province and his army on March 1, 49, the formal date of the close of his command. That is to say, an agreement solemnly entered into had been upset by subsequent enactments.

On every ground of equity Caesar had cause to complain. Curio made the most of the grievance. While Aemilius Paullus delayed the debate in the Senate, he harassed Pompey with incessant jibes and accusations and vetoes in the Assembly, pointing out that this new precisian about the constitution had himself broken every article of it, and had been simultaneously consul and proconsul. He proposed, no doubt at Caesar's instigation, that both Pompey and Caesar should lay down their provinces – to which Pompey could not assent. It was now clear to everybody that the contest was being narrowed to a personal issue – no longer radicals and conservatives, Populares and Optimates, but Caesar and Pompey. In June the Senate decided that each should give up one legion for the Parthian war, and Pompey accordingly requested Caesar to return him the legion lent in 53. Caesar at once complied, but no more was heard of Parthia, and the two legions were detained by Pompey in Italy. He had begun to mass his forces.

The breach came early in 49. Both consuls were senatorians, but among the tribunes was Mark Antony, one of Caesar's lieutenants in Gaul. On the first day of the year, Curio, the ex-tribune, appeared in the Senate with a letter from Caesar, of which the consuls tried to prevent the reading. Caesar had already, from beyond the Alps, sent proposals for peace, and now he declared his final terms. They were moderation itself. He offered to give up Transalpine Gaul and eight of his legions if he were allowed to retain Cisalpine Gaul and Illyria with two – an arrangement which was only to last till he entered upon his second consulship. Further, he declared that he was ready to lay down his command if Pompey would do likewise. He asked not more but less than he had been granted at Luca. It was the last hope of peace, and Cicero, who had just returned after a strenuous year as governor of Cilicia, thought – and he claimed to speak for the majority – that the terms should be accepted. But Pompey's slow and irresolute soul had been stiffened into obstinacy, and he would have none of them. He let his supporters know that the moment for action had come. The Senate decreed that Caesar must give up his province by March 1 of that year on pain of being proclaimed a public enemy. The Caesarian tribunes vetoed the resolution, but on January 7 the Senate declared a state of war, enjoining the consuls to see that the republic took no hurt. A general levy was ordered, and the treasury was put at Pompey's disposal. Mark Antony and Quintus Cassius escaped from Rome in the disguise of peasants and fled towards Caesar's camp at Ravenna.

While the tribunes were speeding along the Flaminian Way Caesar had come to a decision. His enemies had taken the initiative in opening the floodgates of civil war. He himself had respected the law which Pompey had scorned, but the moment had come when all laws had little meaning. He had already sent across the Alps for the rest of his troops, and on January 10, as soon as the news arrived from Rome, he called together the soldiers of the Thirteenth legion, and unfolded to these young men of north Italy, whose cause he had always championed, the nature of the crisis and the reward which was preparing for the conqueror of Gaul. Their enthusiasm convinced him of the loyalty of his army. That afternoon he sent off secretly an advance party to seize the Italian border-town of Ariminum (Rimini) – his first act of revolution. He attended the local games and dined quietly with his staff, and then after dinner slipped off with a small retinue and crossed the little brook, called the Rubicon, which was the Italian frontier. We may reject the legends which grew up later about his hesitations and doubts on the brink of the stream and his relapse into antique superstition; such was not the nature of the man, and in any case he had taken the irrevocable step hours before when he sent off his advance guard to Ariminum. But Asinius Pollio may well have heard him, as he crossed, murmur the tag from Menander, 'Let the die be cast.'

There is no record of Caesar's thoughts during these last fateful days, but it is permissible to guess at them. He was most deeply anxious for peace. On this point the evidence is overwhelming, both from his deeds and from the admissions of his opponents. He had gone to the extremest lengths in concession, and had been willing to put himself well within the danger of his enemies. He knew the weakness of his own position. The complex party machine which he had built up in Rome had no meaning in civil war. What availed it that he had the urban rabble on his side if to all the substantial classes his name was anathema? The old nobility, the bureaucracy, the capitalists looked upon him as a menace to the state and to their own fortunes, and many hated him with the vindictiveness which the dull always show towards a genius beyond their comprehension. Even among honest folk his name stank because of the tools he had been forced to use. Pompey had seven legions in Spain and the better part of ten in Italy, he had the authority for a general levy, and he had all the financial resources of the state, including the rich provinces of the East. Caesar himself was poorer than when nine years before he had gone to Gaul, for he had spent all the fruits of his victories on his largesses in Rome. He had, it was true, nine veteran legions, of magnificent fighting quality, but they were now reduced in numbers and wearied with long campaigns. Could he count on their loyalty if he embarked on a struggle with the embattled forces of that commonwealth of which they had hitherto been the servants?

They longed for peace, all Italy longed for peace, and the man who forced on war would incur a universal odium. What matter that this man had been shamelessly treated! Plain people would look only at the fact that he was defying the established government of the republic.

In the face of such handicaps Caesar was forced to his decision in the first place on personal grounds. He was literally fighting for his life. If he submitted he was a doomed man. When later he walked among the dead at Pharsalus, he was heard by Pollio to murmur to himself, 'This is what they brought me to. If I had dismissed my armies, I, Caesar, would have been condemned as a felon.' But with such a character personal fear plays only a little part; more grave was the ruin of a career and the downfall of the ambitions of a lifetime. By the labours of thirty years he had made for himself a dominant position in the state, and this was now in jeopardy. He had begun by playing the obvious game for its obvious prizes, careless what weapon he used, but as he moved upward his motives had changed. Certain attachments he had always cherished, the sentimental attachments of his kin and his party, but slowly he had acquired deeper and prouder loyalties. Unless everything were to go by the board, he must be prepared to 'put it to the touch to win or lose it all,' to make the supreme effort of courage and to stand alone.

Gradually the conviction must have forced itself on his mind that there was no way but revolution. Senatorial government was now in itself a revolutionary thing, for it played fast and loose with the law and disregarded utterly the spirit of the constitution. This slovenly lawlessness could only be checked by a nobler and wiser kind. Pedants still prated about the preservation of the republic, but there was no republic to preserve. With his clear insight Caesar looked upon the life of Rome and saw its rottenness. The old regime had gone beyond hope of recall, and for a Periclean democracy the first conditions were wanting. He knew the Optimates, for he belonged to them by birth; he knew the bourgeoisie, for he had been at various times its bogey and its darling; he knew the mob, for he was still its leader. In no class was there any sound tradition of civic liberty and decency, and the ancient constitution which formally survived was a mere parody of government. He was not yet confident as to the right course for the future, but he was very clear that there must be a wholesale demolition of rubbish and a rebuilding from the foundations.

But the creed towards which he was feeling his way was not negative only. If Rome was moribund, her domains had still the stuff of life. In his wars he had learned something of their people, and he believed that there was material there for the making of a great nation. The East he did not know, but he could speak at first hand for the West – for Italy, for Spain, for the land beyond the Po, for the wide spaces of the North. He had now a conception of a different type of empire – an empire of vigorous local life and culture, self-governing under some new and more generous polity, not merely a territory of Rome, but Roman in a truer sense than the city by the Tiber.

There things were still in the lap of the gods. In the meantime there was the urgent crisis before him, the duty of following his star, of bringing order into chaos by the force of his genius and in the last resort by his sword. If the future depended upon one man, that man would not be found wanting. It was a true instinct which led later ages to regard the crossing of the Rubicon as a decisive moment in the history of the world.

CHAPTER 9

The Conquest of the World

In four years Caesar battered down the walls of the old Rome and began the building of the new, and in these years, incidentally, he conquered the world. He moved about the globe like a fire, habitually daring extreme occasions, taking the one chance in a thousand and succeeding, careless of life and fortune, conducting himself like one who believes that he has a divine mission and that the gods will not recall him till it is fulfilled. His work may well seem to reach the extreme compass of what is possible for a mortal spirit. But he could not have achieved it unless the fabric he assailed had been rotten and the men he fought only relics and simulacra. He is the one living man among a medley of phantoms.

At dawn on January 13 Caesar occupied Ariminum. He straightway sent Mark Antony across the Apennines to occupy Arretium (Arezzo) and so protect his flank, while he marched south along the Adriatic, taking the little coast towns. A message from Pompey induced him to make another effort for peace; he wrote begging for an interview, and proposed that they should both disarm, that Pompey should proceed to Spain, and that he himself should give up his *imperium* and go to Rome to stand for the consulship. For some weeks he hoped and toiled for conciliation, but Labienus, his chief lieutenant, had gone over to

Pompey and had filled his mind with tales of the weakness of Caesar's command, and Pompey hardened his heart.

Caesar's aim was to manoeuvre his opponent into a corner where he could force upon him a personal meeting, for he believed that if he could break through the cordon of senatorian advisers he could make Pompey see reason. But Caesar's speed had been too successful, for it scared his enemies out of reason into panic. He was the 'man from the north,' with behind him all the prestige of that dim land from which in past times conquerors had marched to the gates of Rome. Pompey might have a greater weight of numbers, but Caesar had the spearhead. Moreover, they knew in their hearts that Caesar had been tricked and insulted and had many accounts to settle. So every road running south and east from Rome was thronged with fleeing politicians and all the classes whose consciences were bad and who had much to lose; they did not even tarry to empty the state coffers. Among them went Cicero, much out of temper and with no illusions left about Pompey and the senatorians.

Presently Pompey recovered his wits. He may have meant at first to make a stand at Brundisium and challenge Caesar's small force. But he did not trust his troops, and he found his new levies hard to mobilise in the winter weather. He went first to Capua, and then to Luceria in Apulia, which was on the road to Brundisium. At Corfinium, eighty miles to the north-west, Domitius Ahenobarbus was left to collect an army. But Caesar was upon him, and on February 20 he took the place, sent back Domitius to his master, and enlisted the senatorian levies under his own standard. He still hoped to bring Pompey to book in Italy, and force him and the Senate to conclude a reasonable peace. He took no man prisoner, and dismissed every Pompeian who fell into his hands with friendly messages. 'My method of conquest,' so ran his published declaration, 'shall be a new one; I will fortify myself with compassion and generosity.'

Pompey, who had now been joined by the whole senatorial debating society, and by all the rich and timid who saw even in this broken reed the only support for their fortunes, was in no mood either to stand or to treat. He had decided to leave Italy and to fight in the East, which was his old campaigning ground. His vanity had been so deeply wounded that he was ready for war to the uttermost. A fleet was collected at Brundisium, and, when Caesar arrived there on March 9, part of the Pompeian army had already sailed. Caesar tried to blockade the remainder and again sought an interview with Pompey, but with the loss of two ships Pompey made his escape and there were no transports in which to follow him.

Italy was now in Caesar's hands, for in two months his deadly swiftness had broken up or immobilised ten legions. But Italy lay between two fires, great armies in Epirus in the East and in Spain in the West. Caesar hastened to Rome to patch up some kind of interim government. He implored the senators who had stayed at home to help him to restore order and to carry on the administration. He strove to allay the fears of the well-to-do and made an arrangement about debts which disappointed his more impecunious supporters. He took possession of what funds remained in the treasury, and left Lepidus, the praetor, as the chief officer of government in the city, and Mark Antony, the tribune, in command of the Italian troops. This latter was an unfortunate appointment, for it was by his association with Antony that Caesar's reputation has been most seriously smirched. Gross in habit, a savage in appetites, almost illiterate (he wrote vile Latin), without the rudiments of statesmanship, he had no gifts as a leader except the 'Caesariana celeritas,' which in his case was often misdirected; and there is good reason to suspect at various times his loyalty to his master.

Then, having decided that if one is between two fires it is well to begin by quenching the nearer, Caesar started early in April for Spain. 'I go,' he said, 'to meet an army without a general, and shall return thence to meet a general without an army.'

The key-point of Massilia (Marseilles), defended by Domitius Ahenobarbus who had been released at Corfinium, declared for

Pompey, and Caesar left its reduction to Decimus Brutus with a hastily prepared fleet. Then he crossed the Pyrenees to deal with the army of Spain. He found it north of the Ebro at Ilerda (Lerida) on the river Segre – seven legions, to meet which he had six, and a strong force of Gallic cavalry. His aim was to fight a bloodless campaign, since he was fighting against Romans, and to manoeuvre the enemy into a position where he would be compelled to surrender. In forty days he succeeded, by taking risks which would have been insane except for a general who had a veteran army in which he could implicitly trust. By diverting the Segre he forced the Pompeians to move south to the Ebro, overtook them on the march, drove them into a hopeless position from which they were compelled to retreat towards Ilerda, hung on their heels, brought them to a halt, surrounded them, and left them no alternative but surrender. He asked only that they should disband, and he gave them food and their arrears of pay. Hither Spain was now in his hands, and Farther Spain, under Varro the antiquary, presently made its submission. Early in September he was at Massilia, which had yielded to Decimus Brutus. Only in Africa was there any setback, where Curio had been beaten by Juba the Numidian king, and slain.

Caesar had now under his control all of Italy, Spain, Gaul, Sardinia, and Sicily, and the food supply of the capital was thus assured. He had been made dictator in order to hold the consular elections, a post which he filled for eleven days, till he was duly nominated to his second consulship. After seeing that the full citizenship was granted at last to the inhabitants of Transpadane Gaul, he turned his face eastward, and by the close of December was ready to embark at Brundisium. A lesser man would have been content to control the West and remain in Italy on the defensive, but Caesar saw that this would mean a splitting up of the empire, and he was not minded to let any part of the Roman domains slip from the hands of the master of Rome. His duty was to seek out and beat his enemy before he did further mischief.

Meantime Pompey, with his retinue of patricians and capitalists, was comfortably entrenched on the Illyrian coast at Dyrrhachium (Durazzo). He had got himself an army, and the twin points in his policy were the control of the sea and of the vast recruiting grounds of the East. He had a magnificent fleet under Bibulus, and Caesar could scarcely lay his hand even on transports. He did not believe that his enemy could follow him, and his intention was to return and reconquer Italy in the spring. The sea gave him the strategical initiative, and he had all the advantages in numbers and equipment. His obvious course was to take the offensive, but, confused by the divided voices of his entourage, he remained supine. Caesar, with as many troops as he could find shipping for, escaped the watching Bibulus, and on January 5, 48, landed a hundred miles south of Dyrrhachium and pushed northward to Apollonia. He was clinging to an unfriendly coast, with a dubious hope of supplies and precarious communications.

What followed is one of the most audacious episodes in military history, in which Caesar suffered the second defeat of his career. He fortified a camp on the south side of the river Apsus, while Pompey sat on the opposite bank. Mark Antony brought over the rest of his legions, and managed to land them at Lissus, well to the north of Dyrrhachium. Caesar by a flank march joined him before Pompey could intercept him, and the latter fell back on Dyrrhachium. Caesar established himself to the east of the town, and by a line of circumvallation penned in Pompey between himself and the sea. But twenty thousand men could not imprison fifty thousand, and Pompey, by a sudden assault at a weak point of the enclosing lines, inflicted upon his opponent a severe defeat. Caesar is said to have declared that his antagonist could have won the campaign at this point if he had known how to command.

Retreating to Apollonia, Caesar waited to see what the enemy proposed to do. The right course for Pompey was to make forthwith for Italy, which would have fallen helpless into his hands; in that event Caesar intended to march round the head of the Adriatic and fight from the base of Cisalpine Gaul. Or he might join his father-in-law, Metellus Scipio, who was bringing reinforcements from Syria, and whom Caesar had sent off two legions under Domitius to intercept. Pompey chose the latter course and turned east along the Egnatian Way to meet Metellus. Domitius brought off his legions just in time, and joined Caesar in the north-west corner of the plain of Thessaly. Pompey, united with Metellus, turned southward, intending to wear down Caesar's small army by manoeuvring and to use his powerful cavalry to cut off its supplies. But Labienus' talk about the poor quality of Caesar's men had done its work, the young bloods of the aristocracy insisted on putting an immediate end to their detested enemy, so at Pharsalus Pompey at last offered battle.

Pharsalus, one of the decisive actions of the world, has no great tactical interest. It was a victory of veterans of uniform type and training against a motley levy, of resolved genius against irresolute mediocrity. Pompey's plan was to outflank Caesar's right – his shieldless side – with his 7000 cavalry, but Caesar anticipated it, and placed a fourth line of six cohorts there in special reserve. There, too, he placed his small but efficient body of horse, and the unconquerable Tenth legion. After addressing his men he ordered the charge. The two centres were at once interlocked, and when the Pompeian cavalry swung to the outflanking movement they were met by Caesar's infantry reserve, who used their javelins as stabbing spears and routed the horsemen. This decided the issue. Caesar flung in his fourth-line supports; the enemy broke, fled to his camp, which was soon stormed, and surrendered in masses. Pompey himself galloped to Larissa and thence to the coast. He had lost 15,000 killed and wounded and 24,000 prisoners. At Mytilene he took ship for Egypt, and was murdered as he landed at Pelusium, a melancholy end for a just man who had stumbled upon a destiny too great for him. The time was now the late summer.

Caesar followed hot-foot on the trail, for it was not his way to leave a task half done. At Alexandria he heard the news of Pompey's death, and discovered that he had stepped into a nest of hornets. The children of Ptolemy Auletes were fighting for the throne, and he found himself involved in a squalid strife of eunuchs and parasites with little more than 3000 legionaries behind him. Once again, as at Dyrrhachium, he was clinging desperately to a hostile shore without supports. The conqueror of Pompey was besieged all winter in Alexandria, and it was not till the end of March 47 that he was relieved by the young Mithridates of Pergamos, and Cleopatra and her younger brother were placed together on the throne. To that winter belong many strange tales. He had an affair with Cleopatra and delayed in Egypt three months after the arrival of Mithridates, though the affairs of the whole world clamoured for his attention. He is said to have sailed with her far up the Nile, and to have dreamed of penetrating to its mystic sources between the hills Mophi and Crophi. That may well be true, for he was always an ardent geographer and avid of new lands; over a man, too, who for eleven years had led the life of the camp, the wit and beauty of that supreme enchantress may have cast a spell. She had a son during the year whom she fathered upon him, and whom Augustus afterwards put to death as an impostor. Caesar's friends disbelieved the tale of Caesarion's paternity, and later ages are free to decide as they please.

But the delay, whether due to Cleopatra or to the necessity of settling Egyptian affairs, gave the embers of opposition time to blow to a flame, and there was mischief afoot in Rome, in North Africa, and in Spain. Caesar left Egypt in June, marched north through Syria, and in a swift and brilliant campaign crushed the insurrection of Pharnaces, the son of the great Mithridates. Then at last he set out for home after an absence of twenty months. At every point in his journey he settled local problems on a basis over which he had long pondered. When he landed in Italy, he met the disillusioned Cicero, whom he sent off to his books with friendly encouragements. In Rome he spent three arduous months. He had been made dictator, and so had the whole administration on his shoulders, and Mark Antony had let things go wildly wrong. Caesar devised a practical solution of the urgent question of debtors and creditors, and quelled a mutiny among his troops by addressing them as 'citizens' instead of as 'fellow soldiers.' Then in the middle of December he set out for Africa, for there the senatorian remnant had massed for a last stand. He went by way of Sicily, where in his eagerness to be gone he pitched his tent within reach of the sea spray.

On the first day of the year 46 he landed in Africa to begin what was to be the most difficult campaign of the civil war. A third time he had flung himself into an unfriendly country with inadequate forces, and, since these forces were mostly new recruits, he had first of all to train them. He was fighting against desperate men, inspired by Labienus, the ablest of his old marshals, and against the craft of their Numidian allies. It was not till early April that he received the rest of his army and was able to offer battle. He invested the town of Thapsus, and the enemy, in an attempt to relieve it, was drawn into a field action. That day Caesar seems to have had an attack of his old ailment, epilepsy, and after the enemy was broken the fight passed out of his control. The Pompeians had shown extreme brutality, his legionaries had many scores to settle, and he was unable to prevent that which he had always laboured to prevent, a butchery of Romans. He moved on to Utica, where Cato was in command. Cato had no power either to stay the rout of fugitives from Thapsus or to defend the place; he did his best to arrange for the embarkation of the garrison for Spain, and then, after reading in the *Phaedo* of Plato, fell upon his sword. So died one who had lost his way in the world, and had retired inside the narrow fortalice of his own self-esteem.

Numidia was added to the Roman domains, and placed under Sallust the historian, and in July Caesar was back in the capital. There he had to go through the wearisome business of celebrating grandiose triumphs, and to take up the heavy burden of the still chaotic government. 'We are slaves to him,' Cicero wrote with startling acumen, 'and he himself to the times.' What he did in Rome during the next six months we shall see later; one thing was the reform of the calendar to make it conform with the solar year, and this meant that the year 46 had to be extended to four hundred and forty-five days. In the intercalary period he fought his last battle. Pompey's son Gnaeus and Labienus had raised the standard of revolt in Spain, and they must be dealt with before the empire could have rest. It was an enterprise in which even the Roman conservatives wished him well. They had no desire to come under the tyranny of a savage like the young Pompey; as Gaius Cassius said, if they were to have a master they preferred the 'old and gentle one.' The campaign, conducted by both sides with intense bitterness, lay in the valley of the Guadalquivir around Cordova and southward, to the foothills of the Sierra Nevada. At Munda, on March 17, 45, came the deciding battle, the sternest of all Caesar's actions except Alesia. It was not till evening, after a long day of silent and desperate bloodshed, that the Pompeians broke. No quarter was asked or given, Labienus and the young Pompey perished, and the bodies of the slain invested the little town like a rampart. His great-nephew, a boy of eighteen, Octavius by name, accompanied Caesar, and on that day first acquired his hatred of the blundering folly of war.

There was peace now on earth, though in the Far East the thunder-cloud of Parthia was still dark. All that summer was spent in arranging the affairs of Spain and Gaul, and Caesar did not recross the Alps till September. Meanwhile in Rome plebiscites and senatus-consults heaped fresh honours on the conqueror, and men held their breath to see what the master of the world would do with his winnings.

CHAPTER 10

Facts and Visions

In the six months left to Caesar of life two major tasks filled his thoughts. Crassus had bequeathed him the Parthian problem as a bitter legacy, and the defeat of Carrhae must be avenged before Rome could be securely mistress of the world. This was more than a mere incident of frontier defence, for he wished to make the East as Roman as the West, and to revive under the Roman eagles the glory of its ancient culture. He had dreams of rebuilding its famous cities and of planting new colonies on the Euxine and the Aegean. Moreover, for his imperial reconstruction he needed money, and the East was still the world's treasure-house. His enemies whispered that he meant to move the centre of power out of Italy, and that not Rome, but Alexandria or Ilium, would be the future imperial capital.

Honours were showered on him, beyond prudence, if not beyond reason. He was so indisputably the master of the world that his friends laboured to devise emblems of his mastery, while his foes were extravagant in their honorific proposals in order that the recipient might be held up to ridicule. Caesar early made two of his purposes clear. He did not mean to perpetuate the military dictatorship, and he began to disband his legions; he desired to establish the rule of one man, so he treated the Senate as no more than an advisory council of state. For the rest, he accepted what was pressed upon him with ironical complaisance, for he held that no titles could increase or detract from the reality of his power. Consul, dictator, censor, *pater patriae,* Imperator for life – these distinctions added nothing to one who was in fact monarch.

It would have been well for him had he been more fastidious about such baubles, for names may have a terrible potency. There were some, friends and foes, who would have had him called king, and no doubt the title would have been useful in his coming campaign in the East. He declined it, for he realised that kingship was no exact description of the place he had won for himself, and that in Roman minds it was cumbered with heavy prejudice; but he refused without conviction, and thereby planted many seeds of suspicion. Rome saw an oriental bias in a mind which was always truly Roman.

What seems to us the more extravagant honour, the approach to deification, really mattered less – his image carried in the solemn procession of the gods, his statue in the temple of Quirinus with the inscription *Deo Invicto,* the new gild of the Luperci Juliani. The idea of the man-god was familiar to the East and not unknown in Rome, for quasi-divine honours had been paid to Scipio Africanus. The ancient state was also a church, and a saviour of the state attracted naturally a religious veneration. Posidonius had made room in his teaching for the deification of rulers, and Posidonius was the fashionable philosopher of the Roman intellectuals, while the cosmopolitan populace saw nothing in the conception to alarm them. Caesar, sceptic and realist, shrugged his shoulders and let popular folly have its way. But he may have seen in it something which might be of use to the empire of which he dreamed. The Greek city-states had failed because they had no ultimate mystical point of unity; they had been too rational, and the rational always invites argument. If the world needed a single ruler, it might be well if that Imperator were also made *divus,* by the foresight of the wise as well as by the superstition of the vulgar.

The urgent task which confronted him had to be faced alone. He appointed the occupants of the regular offices – too cavalierly perhaps, for they had little meaning for him in that strenuous hour of reconstruction. He had a multitude of devoted henchmen, but no cabinet, no colleagues whom he could lean upon for counsel. Fourteen years of unremitting toil had worn out his body, though they had not lowered the vitality of his mind. His health was broken, and his fits of epilepsy were becoming too frequent. Yet, as happens sometimes to a man in middle life who finds himself after long absence back in a familiar world, there was a curious return of youthful interests, as if he longed to resume before it was too late some of the pleasures which he had so long forsworn for ambition. He dined out much, and talked freely; too freely, for his heavy preoccupations made him forget his old tactical discretion. He lived carefully, and an innocent vanity seems to have revived in him. He liked the permission granted him to wear everywhere his laurel wreath, for it concealed his growing baldness, and he was proud of his high red leather boots, which were a tradition of the ancient Alban kings. He had taken to literature again, and amused himself with pamphlets on grammar and style, of which he was a fastidious critic, preferring the dry Attic manner to the more Corinthian rhythms of Cicero; and he published a reply to the numerous eulogies of Cato, which Cicero praised. Cleopatra had come to Rome with a vast oriental retinue, desiring to share the throne of the master of the world, and Roman gossip made Caesar once again her devout lover. It is more likely that the Queen of Egypt's presence was less of a delight than an embarrassment; for such pleasures he was too busy and too weary.

For in the last months of his life he was engaged on no less a task than the remaking of the world. For years he had been pondering the matter, as Napoleon in his Eastern campaign had pondered the reconstruction of France, and it was now his business to put into concrete shape the scheme which he had devised among the African sands and the Illyrian glens and by the reedy watercourses of Gaul. It is not easy to decipher the blurred palimpsest which is all that remains to us, but some of the original script may still be read.

On one point he was adamant – the old constitution had gone for ever. To revive the substance of the republic, as Cicero wished, was beyond the power of man, and to have restored its forms would have been a piece of foolish antiquarianism and a plain dereliction of duty. Caesar was no iconoclast, but he was a little impatient of the trivial, and did not see the value of an occasional condescension to human weakness. The Senate, the old rock of offence, was largely increased in numbers; he may have intended to make it a council representative of the whole empire, but for the moment, while he treated it with respect, he kept it powerless. The Optimates were quietly set aside, though he seems to have had in mind the building up of a new patriciate, based upon the historic houses. But the cardinal matter was the creation of a system under which the sovereign power should be in the hands of a single man, for it seemed to him that no other plan could save the world from anarchy. He was such a man, and, having no son of his body, he looked to his great-nephew to continue his work, for an elective principate was impossible in the then confusion of things. The old Roman *imperium* seemed the natural means by which the new supreme power could be grafted on the state. He aimed at a civil commonwealth, but it was proof of the difficulties of the task that the word which best described the new sovereign was one associated with military command.

Having determined the central power he turned to the details of government. He began the codification of the laws which Hadrian was to complete, notably the praetorian edicts embodying that *jus gentium* which was valid for all free citizens of the empire. He dealt drastically with the scourge of usury, and extricated many honest men from the toils of debt; protected Italian agriculture; extended the bounds of land settlement; suppressed extravagant luxury; abolished the farming of the provincial taxes; in a word, put into effect all that was valuable in the policy of the earlier democrats, while, by the introduction of a means test for recipients, he lessened the evils of the corn dole. He had dreams of restoring the family discipline of an earlier Rome, and there is evidence that, like Augustus, he wished to revive the ancient cults of the Italian soil – 'Pan and old Silvanus and the sister nymphs' – for he had a tenderness for all deep-rooted simplicities. He sought, too, to develop the material resources of his domain, not only to rebuild Carthage and Corinth and drive a ship-canal through the Isthmus, but to drain the Pontine marshes, construct a great port at Ostia, carry roads through the Apennines, and make Rome a city worthy of her fame.

Many of these projects might have been fathered by any aedile of genius. The largeness of Caesar's grasp is to be seen rather in his fundamental policy of empire. His first principle was decentralisation. Rome was to be now only the greatest among many great and autonomous cities. He passed a local government act for Italy which was the beginning of a municipal system, one of the best of Rome's creations, and he proposed to apply its principles throughout the empire, so that the Roman citizenship should be free to all who were worthy of it. The Imperator should nominate the provincial governors and thereby take responsibility for their competence and honesty. The empire was to be rebuilt on a basis of reason and humanity, and, while local idiosyncrasies were to be preserved, the binding nexus would be Roman law and Roman civilisation. He was well aware that government by the consent of the governed was not so much a moral as a physical necessity, and he believed that only by giving to the parts order, peace, and a decent liberty could that consent be won. For sound administration he must have an expert civil service. Already in Gaul he had trained a great staff of competent personal assistants, and now he laid the foundations of that imperial bureaucracy which for four centuries was one of the buttresses of Roman rule.

Such was Caesar's scheme of empire, inspired by the two principles of the ultimate sovereignty of one man and of wide local liberties, and on it the later edifice was built. Instead of a city and a host of servile provinces there was to be a universal Roman nation, in which the conquered should feel that they ranked with the conquerors, and might exclaim in the words of Thucydides, 'We had been undone had we not been undone.' It is easy to see its defects. There was no certainty of continuance in the repository of the sovereign power. The army, if the sovereign were not a great soldier, might interfere malignly in the conduct of affairs. But it seems idle to criticise it on the ground that it lacked representative institutions. Had these been confined to Rome the old oligarchy would have returned, and with vast distances and slow and difficult transport any worldwide system was strictly impossible. Caesar had to make such bread as his indifferent grain permitted. Nevertheless, he offered his world a new evangel. For the first time in government prejudice was replaced by science and tradition by reason. He made the rule of law prevail, and gave the plain man a new order and a new hope.

His achievement – if we must attempt to summarise it – was first that he was a 'swallower of formulas,' a destroyer of dead creeds and decayed institutions. On the constructive side he gave his country a further lease of life by infusing into her veins the fresh blood of the peoples she had conquered. From the provinces were to come in future days many famous Romans – Virgil from his own Transpadanes; Lucan and Seneca and Martial; the great emperors and soldiers of Spanish, African, Gallic, and Dacian stock; the princes of the Christian church who transmuted the cities of Cecrops and Romulus into a City of God. Again, he gave civilisation a life of five further centuries before the dark curtain descended. The empire fell in the end because of the pressure of the barbarians on its frontiers, and because of the ruin of the middle classes within by insensate burdens, and the degradation of the proletariat into a light-witted pauper rabble. These are the causes which at all times are the ruin of great nations – *de nostro tempore fabula narratur.* Caesar by his conquests staved off the descent of the outland hordes, while by his internal reforms he kept the danger from the urban mob within bounds, and safeguarded productive industry in town and country.

He gave the world a long breathing space, and thereby ensured that the legacy of both Greece and Rome should be so inwoven with the fabric of men's minds that it could never perish. He taught no new way of life, no religion; he had no comfort for the weary and the sick at heart; he was a child of this world, content to work with the material he found and reduce it to order and decency. But he made it certain that the spiritual revelation for which mankind hungered would not be lost in the discords of a brutish anarchy. His standards were human, but the highest to which humanity can attain, and his work may well be regarded as the greatest recorded effort of the human genius.

The man who achieved it – and herein lies Caesar's unique fascination – was no leaden superman, no heavy-handed egotist, but one with all the charms and graces. The burden of the globe on his shoulders did not impede his lightness of step. War and administration never made him a narrow specialist. His culture was as wide as that of any man of his day; he loved art and poetry and music and philosophy, and would turn gladly to them in the midst of his most critical labours. He was the best talker in Rome and the most gracious of companions. There was no mysticism or superstition in his clear mind, but he was not without certain endearing sentimentalities. He was tolerant of other men's prejudices and respected their private sanctities. Combined in him in the highest degree were the realism of the man of action, the sensitiveness of the artist, and the imagination of the creative dreamer – a union not, I think, to be paralleled elsewhere.

But the spell of his intellect was matched by the spiritual radiance which emanated from him to light and warm his world. He could be harsh with the terrible politic cruelty of a society based upon slavery, but no one could doubt the depth of his affections and the general benignity of his character. He had no petty vanity; the *Commentaries* is the most unegotistic book ever written. This man, whose courage in every circumstance of life was like a clear flame, had a womanish gentleness and the most delicate courtesy. He never failed a friend, though his friends often failed him. He was relentless enough in the cause of policy, but he could not cherish a grudge and he was incapable of hate; his dislike of Cato was rather the repugnance of a profound intellect to a muddy and shallow one. In Cicero's words, he forgot nothing except injuries. When Catullus abused him he asked him to dinner, and when an enemy fell into his power he dismissed him with compliments. The meanness and the savagery which are born of fear were utterly alien to his soul. The most penetrating and comprehensive of human minds and the bravest of mortal hearts were joined in him with what is best described in a phrase of Mark Antony's which Dio Cassius reports, an 'inbred goodness'.

His dreams were to be fulfilled, but his immediate work failed, as it was bound to fail, for he was a man of genius and not a demigod. The pioneer is rarely the exploiter, and the man who destroys an old edifice and marks out the lines of a new one does not often live to see the walls rise. Caesar made the empire by preparing the ground for it, but, like King David, he had to leave the building to another. He had aroused too many deep antagonisms to be permitted to complete his task. He was too much above his contemporaries, too far in advance of his age, too solitary in his greatness. Moreover, the world had not yet learned its lesson and the forces of strife were not yet spent. Years were still to follow of anarchy and misery till Rome in utter weariness could accept Caesar's evangel, and a different type of worker could finish his work, the slow, patient 'trimmer' who interwove so cunningly the new with the old that men accepted novelties as common sense. The future was with his great-nephew Octavius, the son of the country banker, now a pleasant modest youth of seventeen. It was given to Augustus to bring into being what Julius dreamed.

During the last months of 45 it was plain that clouds were massing on the horizon. Caesar had pardoned his enemies, but they did not forgive him, and the remnants of the old senatorian faction looked on at his doings in impotent hate. Honest conservatives regarded the new monarchy as an impious breach with a sacred past, and ambitious men like Gaius Cassius felt themselves shamed and overshadowed by Caesar's lonely greatness. The wise youth, Marcus Brutus, Cato's nephew and Servilia's son, had become wiser than ever, and had won great repute, in spite of his notorious avarice, as a repository of the antique virtues. Even Caesar respected him, for he seemed to have a *gravitas* uncommon in that age. Brutus was rapidly becoming intoxicated by the flattery of his friends and by his own brand of rhetoric. Some, too, of Caesar's old companions in arms, like Decimus Brutus and Trebonius, were growing estranged. A general can count more securely on the loyalty of the rank and file than upon that of his marshals, for these are apt to think that his fame has been of their making, and to be jealous of any pre-eminence which they do not share. Moreover, there was widely diffused in Roman society an uneasiness about what the future might hold, and fear about the Parthian campaign. Men saw moving from the East the spectre of an oriental monarchy in place of the Rome which they knew and loved.

Caesar was aware of these hidden fires, but he refused to deviate one step from his course. He would have no bodyguard, and walked unattended and unarmed in the streets, for it was better, he said, to die like a free man than to live like a tyrant. When his friends warned him of conspiracies he smilingly put them by. The honourable fatalism, which is necessary for any great achievement, was now, as always, his philosophy; the gods would not send for him until his task was finished, for only on that presumption could life be lived. But it is clear that in these last months he thought often of death. Sometimes a great weariness overcame him, and he was heard to say that he had been long enough in the world. On the night before his end the conversation turned on the best kind of death, and he said abruptly, as if he had long pondered the matter, 'a sudden one.' But he would not change his habits or take any precautions, for such would have been beneath his Roman pride. Perhaps, too, in a mind so prescient there lay another reason. He may have come to realise that the task he had set himself could not be completed by his hands, but that its success would be assured if it were sealed with his blood. 'For where a testament is, there must also of necessity be the death of the testator.'

CHAPTER 11

The End

On the 19th of March 44, Caesar was to leave for the East on his Parthian campaign. On the Ides, the 15th, a meeting of the Senate was called to make the final arrangements, and this was the occasion which the conspirators selected for their deed. A month before at the Wolf-festival, the Lupercalia, Caesar had been offered a crown by Antony, and when he had put it aside there had been shouts of 'Hail, O King!' although the main plaudits were for the rejection. What had to be done must be done at once, for the Roman people were plainly in a divided mood. It was resolved that the Senate's meeting was the proper occasion, since the whole body of senators would thus be compromised, and the murder would have the colour of a ceremonial act of justice. On the night of the 14th the conspirators dined with Cassius. Some proposed that Antony and Lepidus also should die, but Marcus Brutus objected that this would spoil the sacrificial character of the deed. Cicero was not admitted to their confidence, being regarded as too old, too garrulous, and too timid. Caesar supped with Lepidus, and at the board sat his old marshal, Decimus Brutus, now one of the leaders of the plot.

The morning of the Ides was fair spring weather. It was the festival of an ancient Italian deity, Anna Perenna, and the Field of Mars was thronged with the commonalty of the city, dancing, and drinking in rude huts of boughs. Caesar had a return of his old fever; his wife, Calpurnia, had slept badly and had dreamed ill-omened dreams; the auspices, too, were unfavourable, though he had never set much store by auspices; so he sent Antony to postpone the Senate's meeting. The conspirators, with daggers in their writing-cases, were at the rendezvous at daybreak in the colonnade of Pompey's Curia, and in case of need Decimus Brutus had a troop of gladiators stationed in the adjoining theatre, where a performance was going on. But no Caesar appeared, and presently came Antony with news of the adjournment. The gang were in despair and despatched one of Caesar's former lieutenants to his house to plead with him to change his mind. The mission was successful. Caesar shook off his lassitude, ordered his litter, and just before noon arrived at the Curia.

Trebonius detained Antony in conversation in the porch, for Antony's bull strength was formidable. The dictator entered the house – a little haughty and abstracted, as if his mind were on higher things than the senatorian ritual. A paper had been put into his hands by someone in the crowd, which contained the details of the plot, but he did not glance at it. The senators rose as he advanced and sat himself in his gilded chair. A petition was presented, and the conspirators clustered around him as if to press its acceptance, kissing his breast and seizing his hands. Annoyed by their importunity he attempted to rise, when one of them pulled the toga from his shoulders. This was the preconcerted signal, and Casca from behind wounded him slightly in the throat. He turned and caught his assailant's arm, and in an instant the whole pack were upon him, like hounds pulling down a deer. He was struck in the side, in the thigh, in the face, and his assailants stabbed each other in their blind fury. He covered his head with his gown in a vain effort of defence, but his frail body was soon overpowered, and he fell dead with twenty-three wounds at the base of Pompey's statue.

The deed was done, and Brutus, raising aloft a dripping dagger, cried out to the ashen Cicero that liberty was restored. He began a prepared speech, but there was no one to listen, for the senators had fled. The murderers, still shrieking and babbling in their excitement, rushed out of doors, and one of them lifted up a cap of freedom on a spear and called on the people to revere the symbol. But the streets were empty. The revellers of the Anna Perenna festival had fled to their homes, the booths were closed, the theatre audience had scattered, and the gladiators of Decimus Brutus were looting far and wide. The ominous silence brought some sobriety into disordered minds. Where was Antony? Lepidus and his legion were not far off. Rome seemed to take their deed less as a liberation than as an outrage. They ran stumbling to the Capitol for refuge.

Presently came three faithful slaves, who carried the dead body to Caesar's house, and, as the litter passed, men and women peeped out of their shuttered dwellings, and there was much wailing and lamentation. A little later Brutus and Cassius descended to the Forum to harangue the people, but they found that the listeners received their appeals in silence, so they hurried back to their sanctuary. As the March dusk fell Cicero visited the refugees and did his best to hearten them. He told them that all Rome rejoiced at the tyrant's death, but they had seen the faces in the streets, and disbelieved him. They begged him to go to Antony and call upon him to defend the republic, but he declined, for he knew better than to put his hand in the wolf's mouth.

Meantime, in the home on the Palatine, Calpurnia was washing the wounds of her dead husband, and Antony was grimly barricaded in his house, and Lepidus sat in the Forum with his avenging legion. In the Capitol the liberators continued their feverish council, every man of them twittering with nerves, now expanding in sudden outbursts of rhetoric and self-admiration, now shaken with terror and crying that all was lost... They feared for themselves, but they believed that they had done with Caesar, not knowing that their folly had perfected his task and made his dreams immortal.

BIBLIOGRAPHICAL NOTE

A short sketch does not permit of annotation, and it seemed to me better to set down my own views without arguing about the evidence. For those who may wish to study that evidence I append a short bibliography.

ANCIENT

The chief authorities are the *Orationes* and *Epistolae* of Cicero, the seven books of Caesar's own *Commentarii de Bello Gallico,* and the three books of his *Commentarii de Bello Civili;* the eighth book *de Bello Gallico* and the *de Bello Alexandrino,* probably written by his lieutenant Aulus Hirtius; and the *de Bello Africano* and the *de Bello Hispaniensi,* the work of unknown officers. The *Catilina* of Sallust contains one of Caesar's speeches, and there are references to him in several of the lyrics of Catullus and in some of the fragments of Varro. These, together with the Julian laws contained in the *Corpus Juris Civilis* and the Berlin *Corpus Inscriptionum Latinarum,* are all we have in the way of contemporary sources.

The books by Asinius Pollio and by the Caesarians Oppius and Balbus have disappeared, but their contents were undoubtedly used by later writers. The classic Roman history of Livy (who was born in 59 BC and was therefore almost a contemporary) has come down to us in an imperfect form, and the eight books dealing with the Civil War survive only in a summary. Livy was of the old republican school, and we may assume that his opinions were repeated by subsequent biographers. These obviously incorporate great masses of floating tradition about Caesar, and it is impossible to say what is fact and what is legend. The *Pharsalia* of Lucan (AD 39–65) is the work of a strong anti-Caesarian, and a glorification of Cato. Suetonius (*c*. AD 100), in his chapter on Julius in his *de Vita Caesarum*, shows the same spirit in a more moderate form, and he was followed by Plutarch (*c*. AD 45–127). It is likely that both Suetonius and Plutarch were much influenced Livy. Appian (*c*. AD 138) in his 'Ῥωμαϊκά', is a more objective writer, but he is hasty and careless. A sounder historian is Dio Cassius (*c*. AD 155–235) who attempts some independent valuation of Caesar's character, and writes in a cool detached tone, but he too is demonstrably inaccurate. To these non-contemporary writers who worked on material which is now lost to us there may be added the fragment of Nicolaus of Damascus (in Müller's *Fragm. Hist. Graecorum*) who lived under Augustus, the occasional gossip of Aulus Gellius, and the two books of the *Historia Romana* of Velleius Paterculus, who was praetor under Tiberius.

MODERN

The chief general works on the period are Drumann, *Geschichte Roms* (1834–44: new ed. by Gröbe, 1906); Duruy, *Histoire Romaine* (1881); Mommsen, *Römische Geschichte* (1854–56: Eng. trans., 1894); and Guglielmo Ferrero, *Grandezza e decadenza di Roma* (1902: Eng. trans., 1907). Of these writers Drumann is the safest guide. Mommsen is a historical genius of the first order who has made Roman history live again for the world, but he carries his admiration of Caesar to the point of idolatry, and he is over-fond of drawing inexact parallels with modern conditions. Ferrero has remarkable narrative skill, but he is apt to let his imagination run riot, and his ingenuity is often perverse. A work more limited in scope but admirably judicious and careful is Rice Holmes' *The Roman Republic and the Founder of the Empire* (1923).

The best life of Caesar is that of Warde Fowler (1891). Froude's *Caesar* (1879) is like Mommsen's *History,* the work of a man of genius who weakens an argument, which I believe to be substantially sound, by overstating it. The *Histoire de Jules César* (1865–1866) of Napoleon III contains the results of archaeological research in France up to the date of its publication. All three books are the work of strong admirers. E G Sihler's *Annals of Caesar* (1911) is a useful critical analysis of the evidence. A recent biography on popular lines is Matthias Gelzer's *Caesar der Politiker und Staatsmann* (1921). The case of the moderate conservatives like Cicero will be found in Strachan-Davidson's *Cicero* (1894), and the essay on 'Cicero's Case against Caesar' in vol. v. of the edition of Cicero's *Letters* by Tyrrell and Purser (1897).

Various episodes of the life have been the subject of special monographs. The most important is Eduard Meyer's *Caesars Monarchie und das Principat des Pompejus* (second ed., 1919), which also contains a valuable account of the authorities ancient and modern. The quarrel with the Senate which led to the civil war – a vital point in Caesar's career – has been exhaustively discussed by Mommsen in his *Die Rechtsfrage zwischen Caesar und dem Senat* (1857), and by later writers like Guiraud and Holzapfel. The campaigns have been treated by experts – Napoleon I *(Précis des guerres de César,* 1836), Napoleon III *(op. cit.),* Colonel Stoffel *(Hist. de Jules César – Guerre Civile,* 1887, and *Guerre de César et d'Arioviste,* 1890),* and by the Duc d'Aumale in a celebrated article in the *Revue des Deux Mondes,* May 1858. But so far as the Gallic Wars are concerned everything is superseded by Rice Holmes' encyclopaedic *Caesar's Conquest of Gaul* (second ed., 1911). We still await a synoptic study of Caesar's military genius, such as Captain Liddell Hart has given us for Scipio Africanus.

The busts of Caesar will be found fully treated of in Bernouilli's *Römische Iconographie*. For the Roman machine of government in Caesar's day the reader may consult A H J Greenidge's *Roman Public Life* (1901) and Dr Stuart Jones' chapter on 'Administration' in *The Legacy of Rome* (1923). Roman private life is dealt with compendiously in Marquardt's great *Privatleben der Römer*, and most attractively in Boissier's *Cicéron et ses amis* (1865: Eng. trans., 1897), and Warde Fowler's *Social Life at Rome in the Age of Cicero* (1908). For the background of political and ethical thought during the period, reference may be made to P Wendland's *Die hellenistischrömisch Kultur* (1907), Warde Fowler's *Roman Ideas of Deity* (1914), E Bevan's *Stoics and Sceptics* (1913), and Professor Barker's essay on 'The Conception of Empire' in *The Legacy of Rome*.

No proper understanding of Caesar is possible without some knowledge of the work of Augustus, a figure second in importance only to Julius. For this the reader may be referred to Mommsen, *Provinces of the Roman Empire* (1884: Eng. trans., 1886); W T Arnold, *Roman Provincial Administration* (1906); Stuart Jones, *The Roman Empire* (1908); and Rice Holmes, *The Architect of the Roman Empire* (1928–31).

John Buchan

Gordon at Khartoum

The year is 1883 and Gladstone finds that the cutting of the Suez
Canal has involved Britain irrevocably in Egypt's affairs. General
Gordon, Governor of the Sudan, is sent on a mission to evacuate
Khartoum. He is besieged there for ten months by the Mahdi's
troops and is killed two days before a relief force arrives. This
gripping historical account focuses on the bravery of this great
man.

Grey Weather

Grey Weather is the first collection of sketches from John Buchan,
author of *The Thirty-nine Steps*. The subtitle, *Moorland Tales of
My Own People,* sets the theme of these fourteen stories.
Shepherds, farmers, herdsmen and poachers are Buchan's subjects
and his love for the hills and the lochs shines through.

John Buchan

Oliver Cromwell

John Buchan sets out to redress popular opinion of this English soldier and statesman. His biography achieves that aim, starting with Cromwell's childhood and youth.

Born in 1599, Cromwell was a devout Puritan who, when war broke out, formed his Ironsides. He won the battles of Marston Moor and Naseby and brought Charles I to trial. After establishing the Commonwealth, he suppressed the Levellers, Ireland and the Scots. In 1653, five years before his death, he established a Protectorate.

John Buchan wrote of Cromwell 'He is a soldier now on the grand scale, strategist as well as tactician, statesman as well as fighting man, and it is by this new phase of his military career that his place is to be adjudged in the hierarchy of the great captains'.

The King's Grace

This sympathetic portrait starts with the death of Edward VII and George V's succession. It was a reign that saw many changes including the Union of South Africa, the First World War and the General Strike of 1926.

John Buchan wrote that 'This book is not a biography of King George, but an attempt to provide a picture – and some slight interpretation – of his reign, with the Throne as the continuing thing through an epoch of unprecedented change.'

John Buchan

Montrose

This is a compassionate biography of the legendary Scottish commander, James Graham, Marquis of Montrose. John Buchan describes Montrose's command of the royalist forces during the 1644 to 1650 war with the Covenanters. Montrose's exceptional strength, leadership and military genius are brought to life. Buchan also illustrates an important period in Scottish history, adding his own measure of adventure to this study.

The Clearing House

This anthology of extracts from Buchan's writings is well worth reading for its historical range and wide selection of subjects close to the author's heart. Alongside portraits of Julius Caesar, Cleopatra, Virgil, Cromwell and Sir Walter Scott, to name but five, are lyrical descriptions of landscapes. Buchan's love for the great outdoors comes to the fore in his account of the African veld and in the more domestic *Wood, Sea and Hill*. There are also short essays on fishing, shooting and golf, among other sports.

Printed in Great Britain
by Amazon

34978531R00062